DOWN THE DRAIN WITH JANE

DOWN THE DRAIN WITH JANE

A Memoir of an American Family's Three-Year Stint in Pakistan

Circa 1953-1956

Jane Tessitor Braun

authorHOUSE®

AuthorHouse™
1663 Liberty Drive
Bloomington, IN 47403
www.authorhouse.com
Phone: 1-800-839-8640

Published by AuthorHouse 08/22/2012

ISBN: 978-1-4772-6151-4 (sc)
ISBN: 978-1-4772-6150-7 (hc)
ISBN: 978-1-4772-6149-1 (e)

Library of Congress Control Number: 2012915003

For my children, Judi Rudd, Douglas Tessitor, and Joyce Farnsworth who shared Pakistani experiences with their late father and me, and for Berdina (Hotaling) Warren, our wonderful friend who did so much to help make our stay in Karachi more pleasant.

Contents

CHAPTER ONE

WHERE IN THE WORLD IS PAKISTAN?

It was one of those days. Doug, our nine-year-old son, fell out of a tree and burst into the house with a bloody nose; Joyce, our three-year-old, made her grand entrance plastered from head to foot with lipstick and talcum powder; I was up to my elbows in cookie dough preparing snacks for Judi's Brownie troop due at our house in less than an hour, when the phone rang.

It was Frank. "Hi, Jane," he said. "How's everything?"

"Don't ask," I groaned, and proceeded to tell him.

"What you need are a couple of servants," he answered glibly.

"Great. Send them over."

"Sorry. You'll have to go to them."

"What do you mean, 'go to them'?"

"Simple. How'd you like to go to Pakistan?"

"To WHERE?"

"Pakistan."

"What do you mean?"

"The government has offered us a chance to go to Pakistan for a couple of years." He briefly explained that the Pakistani government had sent an urgent request for assistance in setting up and equipping a soil-mechanics and hydraulics research laboratory. Since his technical engineering background was exactly what they needed, he had received a telephone call from Washington, D.C., asking if he would accept the assignment.

"We'll just be on 'loan' from the Denver Bureau of Reclamation," he added. "Think it over. I'll be home in about an hour and we can talk about it then."

Why not, we wondered. It would be a chance to travel, the children were old enough to gain a lot from such an experience, and we certainly couldn't afford such an outing at our own expense.

"What about schools for Doug and Judi?" I asked.

"We might have to teach them at home, but I understand there is a small American school starting there now. They are using a correspondence system," Frank said.+

"What would we do about Joyce's milk?" Our youngest had a serious milk allergy, and had been forced to drink goat's milk for nearly two years.

'That's no problem. They have goats all over the place. As long as she doesn't have to have a ham sandwich, she'll be all right."

"Why do you say that?"

"The Muslim religion prohibits pork in their diets. Americans might be able to bring it over in cans, however. I'll see about that." Frank, looking thoughtful for a moment then added, "Do you think we should rent the house, or sell it?"

"Well, if we go, we probably should sell. It's a good time—we've outgrown this one."

We agreed, and our discussions continued unabated until we had evaluated every angle, even that of uprooting Judi from baton twirling. At the age of 11 she had won the highest score in the Colorado State Baton Twirling Championship, and now, a few months later and a week past her twelfth birthday, had won the junior championship in a tri-state contest held in New Mexico. After weighing the options, we decided a break away from the pressures of competition might be good for her. In fact, the more we evaluated the pros and cons, the idea sounded fascinating to me, exciting to the children, and challenging to Frank.

But, we argued, we knew nothing about Pakistan—hardly knew *where* it was, only that it was a country in Asia that had been separated from British-held India a few years back because of religious differences. In those days, my impression of India consisted only of a vague conception of turbaned men, sacred cows, and snake charmers.

We gathered all of the printed material we could find in order to acquaint ourselves with the country, its customs and its people. Everything we read was exciting, but the "cheery" government bulletins really threw us. They emphasized that Karachi, Pakistan's largest seaport, was considered a "hardship" post—one of the most difficult ones at that. We were sent a Post Report which advised us that the State Department would furnish us a house, a chowkidar (night watchman), and a mali (gardener,) all of which would be paid for out of an allowance subtracted from Frank's base salary.

The house would be furnished with the basic pieces of furniture, but we were advised to bring any additional pieces that we wanted, such as a sewing machine, and to bring bedding and linens of all kinds as "bedding here is expensive, and not available in the proper sizes and quality." The Report continued, "The charcoal stoves which are built into the homes are somewhat crude, but can be operated efficiently by the local cooks. Kerosene is not rationed, and a kerosene stove would be a very handy item indeed."

"What are we getting into, Mom?" Judi asked anxiously. "Look, here it says 'gas or electric stoves are not used, due to a lack of gas and unreliable electric current, but an electric roaster is used by some families when there is enough current.' Sounds like we'll be living in the dark ages!"

"Better bring lots of candles," Doug quipped, "unless you want to go to bed every night at dark."

"We had better stock up on kerosene lanterns, anyway," Frank said somewhat dubiously. "At least we can bring a car. It says, 'An automobile is practically a necessity.' They recommend 'a Chevrolet, Ford, etc., preferably with a *right-hand drive*! We can manage the right-hand drive all right, but I hope they know cars run on gasoline!" He brightened as he read further. "Well, the houses don't sound too bad—at least they have floors in them. Listen. 'There is no need for a vacuum cleaner as the floors are usually of terrazzo tile or cement, and for the sake of cleanliness, scatter rugs are preferable to large carpets.'"

"I wonder if they have indoor plumbing," I asked.

"Yes, I read somewhere that the houses are equipped with modern plumbing."

"It doesn't sound like it to me," Judi cried. "We won't even have hot water! Listen! It says, 'Many of the homes have no hot water tanks. They aren't really necessary because it is usually so hot that a cool shower feels better anyway.'"

"Yippee! That's great, man," Doug said, jumping up and down triumphantly. "Guess we won't have to bother with baths while we're over there. Great! YIPPEE!"

"That's what you think, son," Frank said. "Sounds like it is going to be so hot that you'll be taking baths three times a day and be glad of it. If there is enough water, that is."

Frank continued studying the Post Report. "We will have to be careful, though. It emphasizes that all drinking water will have to be boiled, and no fruits or vegetables can be eaten unless they are peeled or boiled first."

"Boiled lettuce! Ugh!" Judi said. "And imagine two years without a green salad!"

As we studied the food list, some of our fears were dispelled, others became more profound. The list of foods available on the local market went something like this:

> "Eggs—small, but good.
> Meat—cheap, but not as good as home.
> Nuts—good. Buy in shells.
> Liver—poor. Tough.
> Poultry—good, but inclined to be tough and stringy.
> Veal—not slaughtered legally; sometimes butchered after animal dies of unknown or natural causes."

The list of foodstuffs and equipment needed was not only comprehensive, it was downright depressing. Of the items that could be had locally, only seafood was rated excellent, and was said to be plentiful and cheap in season. Also rated excellent was butter, which could be ordered from Denmark at $1.20 per pound (that was expensive in those days.) Most of the fruits and vegetables listed were comparable to those with which we were familiar. Prices varied according to the season and comments varied according to the mood of the writer.

The Report also said "top" steak was available. *That* was the writer's opinion, not ours, we decided later! The Report verified Frank's earlier statement, "fresh pork, tinned pork, ham and bacon are not available at the local market in Pakistan at any time as pork in any form for Pakistani consumption is prohibited by the Muslim religion." Along with these items, the Report suggested we bring foodstuffs such as flour, brown sugar, granulated sugar, baking powder, cake flour and yeast from the States. Also, "dried milk, canned milk and coffee (concentrated weighs less) should definitely be brought out by all families as these products are expensive and limited on the Karachi market. Foods such as asparagus, soups, peanut butter and vinegar would have to be ordered from the States. Crackers, packed in tins, will stay fresh for several months and are," the Report said, "a welcome change from the commercially baked bread which is often of low quality." There was considerable mention of soaps, polishes, and cleaning supplies, then "due to the scarcity of water, a washing machine which is neither automatic nor semi-automatic is helpful. Bring a package of chlorinated lime (HTH) to make your own bleach."

Suggested clothing requirements consisted of mostly washable cottons, with an emphasis on formal attire—dinner jackets, both white and black, for the men; ballerina and floor length cotton (and other) cocktail dresses and formals for the ladies, as "all late afternoon social affairs are semi-formal, and everything after 6:00 p.m. is strictly formal." Clothing for the children would be summertime wardrobes and, except for the fact that we would have to guess sizes, wouldn't present much of a problem.

It was obvious that we not only would have to stock up on foodstuffs, but we would have to bring almost everything we would need for any eventuality. "Either many things aren't available there, or if they are available, we'll never be able to afford them. The prices seem to be at least three times higher than stateside prices for anything that is imported," Frank said.

Our friends thought we had lost our minds; in fact, some of them told us so. The others were more tactful about it. And there were a few (very few) who admitted envying us the opportunity. Most of these were housewives upon learning that servants were considered an absolute necessity and could be hired, the Post Report said, for 8 cents a day. That sounded good to me, too. HA! We soon learned they were nowhere near that cheap, and the number of servants required, due to the "unofficial" caste system, was exceeded only by the number of headaches they caused. We were warned. The Post Report clearly advised us not to get carried away with the prospect of servants because "although essential, they are usually more trouble than they are worth."

The more we read, the more anxious we became. Consulting with the manager of a neighborhood super market who was stationed for 18 months with the U.S. Air Force in Karachi prior to Partition didn't help very much. He broke out in wild gales of laughter when I told him we were going there. With obvious effort, he controlled himself enough to say, "Oh, it's not so bad. You'll like it once you get used to it," and promptly doubled up howling again.

"Why, hell," he said. "We found bugs as big as coffee cups, and you should have seen the snakes slithering across the floor." In mid-air, he outlined the movements of the snakes with his hands, slapped his thighs, and went into wild guffaws again.

"Do you think we're making a mistake to take the kids there?" I asked Frank.

"No, I don't think so," he said. "I think Ralph is just pulling your leg. We'll just have to be careful. We can't expect it to be like the States. If we use common sense, and realize that everything is going to be different, and accept this fact, we should be able to adjust all right."

We had to admit it was a marvelous conversation piece! We were eating it up—especially Judi and Doug, who were commanding a certain reverence from their classmates at school.

"Gee, you're going to India?" We learned early to say India because in 1953 not many people knew about Pakistan, a country at once only six years new, but thousands of years old.

As soon as the final word came through in July, Frank flew off to Washington, D.C., and I flew downtown to buy "everything" for a family of five for the next two years. It ceased to be a conversation piece for me, and became a tremendous amount of work.

As Frank stepped from the plane in Washington, he was handed orders to waive the usual indoctrination course and proceed immediately to Karachi. At the zero hour, some higher-up got wind of that, and vetoed those plans which meant that he had to stay in Washington for nearly three weeks with nothing to do but cool his heels waiting for the next indoctrination class at John Hopkins to start.

He cooled his heels while I burned! Along with the hundreds of details that had to be taken care of, I was left to sort out a 10-year accumulation of extra lumber and odds and ends that Frank had stored in the basement and garage. I was up to my knees in half-used paint cans and up to my ears in assorted nails. True, it wasn't entirely his fault; he had nothing to say about sitting it out in Washington, but, I growled, "He could at least have discarded his junk in the basement while he was waiting the final word from Washington."

The rest of it I didn't mind doing. It was part of my job and I accepted it as such, even though it became a gigantic task. In addition to taking care of our three children and the usual household chores, I was left to sell the house, car, and furniture; buy and sew clothing for ourselves and our children; plan and purchase everything a family of five would conceivably need for two years; do the packing; see about visas and passports; and oh yes, the shots!

Sandwiched in between all of these duties was a small matter of 13 shots apiece! (Fifty-two in all; Frank would get his in Washington.) We took shots to ward against cholera, typhoid, tetanus, yellow jaundice, small pox and anything else that might come along. We were so well immunized we couldn't have caught a butterfly. But then, we hadn't been to Baghdad!

By this time, letters were flying thick and fast between Denver and Washington—to Denver with bits of information that Frank would pick up about Karachi, and back to Washington with reports of progress. I listed everything I had purchased or planned to purchase. None of this "Why didn't you bring so and so" for me! No, Sir. He could check it right along with me or forever hold his peace. The lists we sent back and forth looked like this:

My list:	Frank's reaction:
1 doz. zippers	2 doz. Zippers are $1.50 each in Karachi.
1 case Wesson oil.	Do we need THAT much?
6 lg. cans baking pwdr.	3 cans. You won't be doing as much baking as you think you will with a kerosene stove.
50 lbs. dried fruits	Gets wormy or moldy too fast. Get more canned fruit.
100 rolls toilet paper	Yes.
6 bottles furniture polish	NO! Are you going to DRINK it?
2 cases concentrated	Sure coffee

Ice skates	Leave them. Don't know if they're useable.
Golf clubs	No. Only one course. It's blacktop with an open sewer running through it.

He added vitamin pills to the medicines and below that, tennis balls, and get those rackets fixed. *YE GODS!* What kind of *VITAMINS* did he think we were getting? We hadn't played tennis in 14 years!

He sent other government bulletins and added appropriate notes such as any executive would: "Send for catalogue—S.S. Pierce & Company, Boston, re food orders; take plenty of soap, call Sam and get 200 lbs. of granulated soap and ship with the lift van; bring plenty of dishes, but not the good stuff; don't forget the tableware." The instructions seemed as endless as the lists. For the kids, "—write to Calvert School in Baltimore for their catalogue. Oh, yes, bring a brush and a small can of paint for Judi's bike."

"Yes, Sir"!

The government listed the items that they furnished, which included a refrigerator. To this, he added, "bring our refrigerator, too!"

I tried to limit my purchases to absolute necessities; but even at that, I understand they are still laughing, all the way to the bank, at that person who bought $600 worth of groceries (quite a sum in 1953) at one fell swoop. They *should* have laughed at that person for being so foolish as to think that those purchases would last two years. We hadn't been in Karachi a month before I was imposing on my closest friend, Berdina Hotaling, to send us "essentials" such as pickles, cocktail snacks and bubble gum. Believe me, if we had had to rely on our initial goods for subsistence, we would have been on a starvation diet for the entire second year and much of the first. I was shocked to realize later how much I relied on my friend. I would send her blank checks and she would send us countless items—either things we had forgotten to bring, or things we "couldn't live without." She was priceless, and I shall never be able to thank her enough for everything she did that helped make our stay more pleasant.

In addition to foodstuffs, I tried to plan proportionate amounts of Kleenex, Kotex and seam binding, as well as Band Aids, girdles and hay fever tablets. Many of the items I bought, we didn't need; the things I didn't buy, we needed desperately and many items that I sold or gave away, such as winter clothing, we wished we had brought along. We had to make a choice and our choice was to bring as little as possible with us with the exception of medical supplies. These we were advised to bring in quantities sufficient for any eventuality. We could have competed with any drug store in Karachi! We had penicillin, Aureomycin, sulfa, potassium permanganate to purify the water, all kinds of ointments, insect repellants, enough Merthiolate to paint a barn, cotton, and even several widths of elastic bandages in case of breaks or sprains. Most of these, we didn't need since it was relatively simple to buy medicines in Pakistan (if they were available, and if we could afford them.) Besides, the doctors always prescribed something we didn't have, anyway.

By this time, our garage looked like a supply depot and I felt like the officer in charge. We had cases and half cases of food and clothing stacked high to the ceiling; transformers, records, a kerosene stove, an electric roaster (bought with green stamps from my grocery spree,) and plastic dishes, to mention just a smattering of the garage's contents.

In spite of the harried confusion, everything was going along remarkably well until we experienced one of Denver's severe thunder storms. The lightning streaked across the sky, spitting at the heavens, the thunder boomed, the hail pelted, and the rain flooded in torrents—underneath the garage door!

Fortunately, no great damage was done, but for the next few days our back yard looked like the neighborhood laundry. I'll bet I'm the only person who has ever hung 96 *BOXES* of Kleenex on the clothesline to dry!

My mind was in such a whirl as our moving date approached, that I consumed a lot of our two-year supply of aspirin the final week or two. A call from the packing house two days before departure was no help, either.

"Could you please give me an estimate of the weight of your household goods?" some woman asked.

How on earth did I know how much they weighed?

"I can't even venture a guess," I told her. "It would only mislead you, because anything I would say would be more apt to be wrong than right."

"Can't you give me *some* idea?" she persisted.

"Well, there really isn't very much, as I have sold most of the furniture, and with the exception of one old washing machine, the refrigerator, and a kerosene stove, there isn't much. Just some clothing and a few odds and ends." I forgot to tell her how much clothing or how many odds and ends—forgot completely about our "supply" depot in the garage! We finally agreed that somewhere between 1,500 and 2,000 lbs. would be a safe guess.

The packers arrived at 8:30 a.m. Saturday. I greeted them with "I'm as ready for you as though you were coming next Tuesday. Come on in."

They looked at me quizzically, then at each other, shrugged, and came in anyway.

By noontime, they began calling the office to say they had run into a bigger job than they had anticipated and couldn't possibly make an afternoon appointment. I noticed that they hadn't brought their lunch (after all, there wasn't much of a load), so I cleaned out the refrigerator. They then ate somewhat dejectedly of salami, bread and cheese, served on a hotcake griddle ((because everything else was packed.) With the help of a neighbor, I found enough beer to help them get through the day. Finally, at 6:30 p.m., Bob, the leader of the three-man team, trudged wearily up the basement stairs.

"Will you please check the house, Ma'am, to make sure we haven't overlooked anything?"

"I wouldn't dare," I answered sheepishly. "I'm afraid I might find something. You'd better go while you have the chance." They still had to unload my automatic washer, dryer and mangle at Berdina and Wayne's house in addition to unpacking the truck that night, which now held an estimated 9,000 lbs. (The actual weight turned out to be 10,000 lbs.) Did I ever feel silly sneaking in the back door of the packing company two days later with a card table, a couple of tennis rackets, a stray shoe, and other odds and ends under my arm.

On September 6, 1953, we tearfully bade farewell to Berdina and Wayne Hotaling, and many other Denver friends, and boarded a non-stop flight to New York, where Frank was waiting for us. It was a thrill to see New York for the first time, and even more exciting when we headed for London three days later. Fourteen hours after leaving New York, including refueling stops at Gander, Newfoundland, and Shannon, Ireland, we arrived in London. We managed to spend a few days sight-seeing in London and Rome before heading for a three-day stay in Baghdad, Iraq.

What a shock it was to have left the splendors of Rome six hours earlier, soaring off on the wings of expectation to "the wonders of the mysterious Middle East" and falling flat on our incredulity into another world—a world blanketed by heat haze, flies and sand dunes. We flew over the Mediterranean Sea most of the route, making two stops to refuel along the way. The Mavraq, Jordan, airport where we made a brief stop, consisted of only a wooden building and several tents. In the distance, some huts and a number of camels could be seen filtered through our blood shot eyes—blood shot because our flight was changed and we had to leave Rome at 4:20 a.m. Our second refueling stop was at the nearly isolated airstrip of Basra, Iraq, in 112-degree heat. When we finally landed at the sweltering Baghdad airport it was 3:00 p.m. and the thermometer registered 114 degrees in the shade.

The American Embassy station wagon, strangely incongruous in a Biblical setting, whisked us along deserted streets to the Semiramus Hotel on Al-Rashid Street. Enroute to the hotel, our worst fears were confirmed as inhabitants of a city came to life following their mid-day siestas. Veiled women and strange-looking men dressed in long, dirty flowing robes and turbaned heads swarmed over the streets and market places. They stared at us as though we had just escaped from the zoo. We, in turn, stared at women washing their clothes in the Tigris River as men urinated and children and pye (wild) dogs played in the same water.

The hotel was fairly comfortable, however, with good food. To our surprise, the menus were in English, and the meals were served on tables bordering a lawn that we entered through a garden of flowers next to the Tigris River. Our hotel rooms were insufferably hot, with ceiling fans stirring hot air as they whirred overhead. The mosquito netting that was draped around our beds made us think we were on a safari, instead of beginning a Middle East adventure.

Frank, on the staff of the U.S. Foreign Operations Administration (FOA) which directed the Point Four program of technical and economic aid to under-developed countries, had been asked to examine a dam in Baghdad. While he did so, we carefully avoided fruit that wasn't peeled, and water that wasn't boiled, but had gorged ourselves with watermelons to quench our thirst. No one had thought to tell us that it was customary for the hawkers to pump polluted water into the melons to make them weigh more! The dysentery we suffered was awful, and certainly did nothing to make our trip into Pakistan three days later tolerable.

As we were leaving for the airport, Frank said, "Karachi can't be this bad, and anything better is all right with me!"

CHAPTER TWO

UNMET, SICK, DISILLUSIONED

The four-engine plane flew like a giant bird, darting in and out amongst the clouds, pecking at stars of unparalleled brilliance.

For the first time in my life I had been frightened by people when I was in Baghdad. Now on the plane, I shivered uncomfortably at the turbaned and Jinnah-capped men who were staring boldly through veiled eyelids at me—the weird American woman. Dark skinned, with Aryan features, fine cheek-bones and full, sensuous lips, they sat next to their pudgy wives who, in turn, sat stoically, glancing now and then at our three children, but more often than not, staring unseeingly straight ahead as though impervious to life about them.

Nearing Karachi, the plane circled the field and began its descent. With a grating jolt, the landing flaps snapped to attention and within minutes, the plane raced down the runway and ground to a halt. We, along with the other weary passengers, unfastened our seat belts and prepared to disembark when we were ordered to remain in our seats.

"Oh, no!" we groaned. Our apprehension had nothing to do with being in an unfamiliar country or its people. It was more basic. The 'john' was closed.

Suffering from the "Baghdad Trots" we were miserable, and had plainly been the star occupants in that little room at the tail of the plane throughout the flight from Baghdad. The delay, we feared, could be calamitous!

Before too long, a spray bomb with a man attached swept down the aisle, spewing disinfectant at the passengers in general and each one in particular before disappearing in a cloud of mist. Disinfected, we wearily disembarked from the plane and were instantly slapped in the face with a sponge of hot humidity.

"Whew! Are we going to live in this hot house for *TWO* years?" Doug complained, wiping the perspiration from his forehead with his sweaty palms.

"You'll get used to it, son," Frank said, looking about uneasily. "I wonder where our ride is? The Embassy said there would be someone here to meet us."

It was 3:30 a.m. The heat was oppressive, and that combined with my intestinal disorder sent Pakistan spinning dizzily before me.

"You'd better sit down," Frank admonished. Gathering the children, who felt no better than I did, I collapsed miserably on the nearest bench while our luggage was being inspected. Seeing our "Special Diplomatic" passports, the inspectors gave our baggage only a cursory examination. Frank closed the bags and we waited. And waited. The airport terminal building was virtually deserted by this time. There were a few employees milling about, but our fellow passengers had quickly scattered and disappeared. I noticed a skinny woman clothed in rags sleeping on her haunches against the waiting-room wall, her outstretched hand in a begging position. Elsewhere around the room we could see dark-skinned natives, dressed only in cloth wrapped diaper-like around their hips, scooting 'duck-walk' fashion around us, cleaning up the previous day's clutter with short-handled brooms that had flexible bristles. "Not even bristles," I determined. "They're only branches from some bushes."

"What a welcome!" Judi said dejectedly. "They probably don't care if we're here or not."

"I want to go home," Joyce whined, clinging to my neck as her eyes puckered and tears fell down her tiny face. She spoke for all of us.

"Didn't you tell them we were coming, Dad?" Doug asked.

"I sent a wire from Baghdad two days ago. There must have been a slip-up somewhere."

Within minutes the airport had cleared except for a handful of seedy-looking natives who were dressed in dirty, baggy trousers and long overblouses, with rags wrapped carelessly around their heads. Most of them wore sandals, but as they were boarding a decrepit-looking bus we noticed some of them were barefoot. Women, whom we presumed to be their wives, looked like walking tents in full, gathered garments with hoods attached. They were covered completely from head to foot. Peering cautiously through crocheted 'peepholes,' they dutifully followed their men onto the bus.

"What are we going to do?" Judi asked anxiously.

"We have no choice. The airport limousine has already left. We'll have to take the bus." Frank nudged us, and falling in behind the natives like sickly sheep, the five of us straggled aboard—too dejected to bleat.

Staring out of the bus window into the muggy darkness of the pre-dawn hour, our 12-year-old became panicky. Clutching Frank's sleeve, Judi asked nervously, "But how do we know where to go, Dad?"

"Someone in Washington said the Beach Luxury Hotel was the best hotel in Karachi. We'll go there." We gave instructions to the driver, which surprisingly he understood, before settling back uneasily, wondering what fate had in store for us this time.

Our disappointment at not being met was keen. Half expecting to be robbed, raped, or having our throats slit from ear to ear, I entertained suggesting an immediate return to the States. But the thought of all of the effort we had gone to up to that point—the buying, the selling, the packing, not to mention the thought of repeating the last part of the trip—settled the point. An immediate return was unthinkable. For better or for worse, we were in another world for the duration.

The bus may have been rickety, but the driver was obliging as he dropped every passenger off at specific addresses. As fate would have it, the Beach Luxury Hotel was at the end of the line. It was too dark to see much of the countryside or city through the bus windows, although we did catch occasional glimpses of rickshaws being pedaled along the nearly empty streets. We also watched in awe as a few camels, with lanterns swinging from their necks, ambled along the left hand side of the road, pulling big buckboards behind them. The driver stopped the bus periodically, patiently waiting to let herds of sheep and other animals walk leisurely across the road, before lurching gamely on his way.

Because seats extended the full length on both sides of the bus, we had a good opportunity to observe the natives, and gave them a good chance to study us. To our fellow passengers, we must have looked like creatures that had crawled out from outer space-wan, bleached and weak-kneed. We thought most of our traveling companions looked old and emaciated, except for a lovely girl across the aisle. She had thrown her facial flap back onto her head, and I was amazed at her youth and her beauty. Appearing to be in her early teens, she had jet black hair, high cheek-bones, a lovely olive complexion, and a softly curved mouth which she quickly hid by pulling the corner of her hood (which we were soon to learn are called 'burquas') with a flick of her slender wrist whenever she caught us stealing a glance in her direction. When she did so, only her serious, luminous dark eyes were revealed.

"What a pity to hide such beauty," I thought.

She seemed to be frightened of the man who accompanied her, and I wondered if he was her husband or her father. He could have been either. He scowled the entire journey, and frequently seemed to admonish her by word or gesture, after which she would instinctively shrink into the folds of her burqua, only to gradually reappear again.

"You've got an admirer staring at you." Frank teased, poking his elbow in my ribs. "He hasn't taken his eyes off of you since we got on the bus." Glancing away from the 'burqua' girl, I was startled to see a pompous, portly individual with thick lips prominently centered on his fleshy face staring (it seemed) right through me.

"He gives me the creeps," I muttered. "I wish I had the security of one of her burquas to crawl into."

Sitting next to him was an older man, bearded, grey and wizened with deep lines mapping a face that mirrored countless years of hardship and abject poverty. He huddled next to a sweeper woman, whose lined face also reflected the hardship that life had dealt her. The only woman on the bus without a burqua, she was also the only one that was colorfully dressed. She was wearing a costume of cotton in a variety of bright colors and patterns, intricately carved, heavy silver jewelry around her ankles, wrists and through her ears, and carried the same sort of short-handled broom that we had seen earlier. She was barefooted, except for three silver rings on her toes, and a number of them on her fingers.

"They act like they're mad about something," Judi whispered.

"Maybe they don't want us on the bus," Doug countered.

"I don't think that's the reason," I answered. "They look so sad. I noticed this about the airplane passengers, too, didn't you? None of them were smiling, and notice these people. They all look so unhappy."

"Probably because it's so late. They look dead tired," Frank said, adding, "We don't look so hot ourselves."

Echoing his sentiments, we were all relieved when the bus careened to a halt in front of the hotel some time later. Jumping out, the driver shook awake the doorman who had fallen asleep against a potted plant. Startled, he leaped to his feet, adjusting his long-plumed turban with one hand while rubbing his eyes with the other. Together the two men unloaded our seven suitcases and deposited them in the lobby. Over the roar of the vanishing bus, I heard Frank asking for a room. It was 4:30 a.m.

"Sorry," the room clerk said with a clipped British accent. "There are no vacancies, Sir."

"Boy, this is our night," Doug exclaimed, jabbing his hands into his pockets and turning away quickly in the hopes that we wouldn't see the tear that had inadvertently escaped and was trickling down his nine-year-old cheek.

"Can't you put us somewhere?" I pleaded, doubling up with stomach cramps. "We've had nothing but trouble since we arrived here, and we're too tired and sick to look for another hotel now." A room clerk eyed us carefully, coughed nervously, then said in his clipped British accent, "Well, I say old chap, I've got one single. You can have it in a bit. When the Pan American pilots leave at 6:00 this morning, we can transfer you to their room."

If he had offered us a cracker box, we would have taken it. Clapping his hands sharply, the manager summoned two porters who appeared to be little more than Doug's age. Dwarfed by the amount of our luggage, the porters led us to a mini-sized room and before they had pocketed their tips and disappeared down the hall, we had crawled into the single bed jammed together like five sardines in a can. No one moved in bed. It wasn't that we didn't want to—we couldn't! Cramped and stiff, we were awakened an hour or so later and transferred to the pilots' suite, which had a bedroom and a sitting room, for (we hoped) a fair amount of rest before we faced the new day.

Fair amount was about the size of it, because at 10:00 a.m. we were awakened by a knock on the door. My stomach gurgled and I groaned as I plunged under the covers, head and all. I was in no mood for social pleasantries. It could have been the Queen of Sheba for all I cared.

Frank rose to answer the door.

"Hello!" a congenial voice said. "Are you Frank?"

Frank nodded, and the stranger introduced himself as Frank's new boss. "I am Forrest Burns," he said amiably, holding out his hand. "We received your wire at the office 20 minutes ago. What time did you get in? I'm terribly sorry we didn't know sooner, as we had planned to meet you."

"It must have come over here by camel back," I muttered to myself as I burrowed deeper under the covers.

Following a brief visit, Forrest arranged to send an office car to pick Frank up at 2 p.m., saying office hours were from 8 a.m. to 12 noon, with a two-hour siesta break because "it's too hot in this country to work at noon time." He left saying his wife would call me later that day, and for Frank to wear cotton pants and a short-sleeved shirt to the office. "We don't even wear neckties to work in this country," Forrest said. After he left, we tried to get back to sleep, but it was hopeless. Wild dogs were howling outside our windows as they scratched their fleas and mangy sores; tiny lizards were scurrying up and down the walls; Joyce was shrieking in terror at the sight of them, and finally, when the third set of sweepers (housecleaners) knocked on our door we gave in, showered, dressed and went downstairs for breakfast.

The dining room was large and airy, with just the right amount of sunlight filtering through windows that dominated two walls of the room. Large ceiling fans were whirring swiftly overhead, and beneath them there were 20 or so tables with clean, white tablecloths and colorful floral centerpieces. Several waiters, dressed in knee-length tunics, white duck trousers, and red banners positioned diagonally across their chests with the hotel's insignia printed thereon, were leaning against the wall. Their uniforms were not unlike our drum major uniforms, but included turbans with resplendent ribbons wrapped around and around, ending with fantailed plumes that rose dramatically like fans into the air.

As we entered the dining room, a waiter rushed to escort us to a table—he was so anxious, we thought he was on commission. He was tall and thin with a handlebar mustache that was handsome on his lean, bronze face. He startled me by grabbing Joyce from my arms, but I relaxed as he paused to rearrange her platinum-blonde curls with his long, thin fingers before seating her. When her food arrived, he fed her every mouthful, and in return, she turned on her eyes like electric lights and he melted visibly before us. That began a friendship, an endearment, that was to last throughout our stay between Amir, the table-bearer and our three-year-old charmer. Every chance he got, he would stroke her white hair. He was not assigned to our table, but whenever he could slip away to feed Joyce, he would do so—and get bawled out and fined for it religiously.

CHAPTER THREE

GETTING ACQUAINTED

After a pleasant breakfast the first day we were in Karachi, we walked outside of the hotel and strolled among the tables that were nestled in the shade of awnings and tropical trees. The day, already hot, was not as humid as it had been upon our arrival a few hours earlier. Beyond the tables and behind the bandstand, the hotel's private barge was docked. As we settled into some bamboo chairs on the barge, we watched a never-ending procession of motley men. They were simply dressed in diaper-like shorts and dirty rags encircling their heads as they coaxed their camels, buffalo and donkeys into the Arabian Sea. When they finished scrubbing their animals, they gained relief from the late morning sun by bathing themselves and splashing and frolicking among the animals in the murky water.

As we reclined in the bamboo chairs, we noticed two men approaching the water's edge astride miniature donkeys, their feet nearly touching the ground. The men rode the donkeys into the water until the water slapped at their buttocks, and then they slipped off of the animal's backs. They tried to pull their donkeys into deeper water. One succeeded, but the other was tugging furiously at a rope that was tied to his beast. The donkey would have none of it. Firmly planted on his haunches, he was resisting in no uncertain terms all efforts of his master to drag him further into the water. The donkey won.

"Guess he doesn't like a bath any more than you do, Doug," Judi teased.

"See, Mom, see!" Joyce said excitedly, pulling on my skirt, as three ugly camels plodded awkwardly up to the edge of the shore. As we watched, the camels, in rocking-chair fashion, dropped onto the horny pads of their fore-knees, then rocked backwards, settling onto the pads behind their knees. Repeating the motion, they swayed forward and backward once again until they were lying flat on the ground. Their riders, sans saddles, jumped down, tugged them to their feet again and led them towards the water by means of a heavy rope that was threaded through holes that had been drilled into their nostrils. As they approached the water, one of the camels let out a scream that sounded like a combination of an elephant's trumpet and a lion's roar, and bit and kicked ferociously at his master. Calming him down with a resounding crack on the rump with the rope, the native dragged him into the water.

"Boy, if I were a camel, I'd go in the water. It looks good in this weather, but I'll bet it isn't very sanitary," Judi said, making a face.

"These people haven't learned much about sanitation yet," Frank said, adding that it was one of the most serious problems the Pakistanis have, and one of the F.O.A.'s biggest challenges is teaching them sanitation.

"Gee, they look mean," Judi said.

"Camels are mean. They are supposed to be the meanest domesticated animal, and the only such animal that never really learns to love his master," Frank said.

"They chew so funny!" Doug tried to mimic the camel who was chewing its cud, sending Joyce and Judi into gales of laughter as he pretended to transfer his 'cud' from one side of his face to the other side as the camels were doing.

"Hey, I thought camels had two humps," Judi said, noticing that every camel there had only one hump.

"They told us in Washington that this type is the Arabian camel. The Bactrian camel has two humps, but three-fourths of the camels in the world are the single-humped variety." Frank said.

"Here comes a cow, or bull, or something," Doug said, pointing toward the sandy beach.

"That's a water buffalo. They won't have to drag him into the water; they'd rather be in water than on land." As Frank spoke, the buffalo sank blissfully into the lukewarm water of the Arabian Sea.

It was nearly 1:00 p.m. when we tore ourselves away from the uninhibited waterfront "bathhouse" and made our way back to the hotel.

As the days wore on, we were pleasantly surprised to find the cuisine at the Beach Luxury Hotel was very good. It was prepared by a French chef who, when sober, accomplished some creditable dishes. We were careful to avoid fried food because much of it was saturated with ghee, a clarified butter popular with the Pakistanis but a cooking fat that was often rancid. There was a lot of variety and most of the food was delicious. All water was boiled or treated with halizone tablets. We ate plenty of rice, potatoes, cauliflower, cabbage, carrots and peas. The seafood in season, especially lobster on the half shell, was as delicious as the Post Report had indicated, although we passed up the specialty the day they served octopus. We enjoyed lamb, chicken, beef and veal (legal or not). We ate cucumbers, apples and pears if we could peel them. Some people ate grapes, but they always washed them in "pinky" water—potassium permanganate—before eating them.

The breakfasts, however, left something to be desired. Rolled oats, dry cereals (served with hot, boiled milk) or eggs and fish cakes were the usual fare. I began ordering eggs, but soon changed my mind because many of them were so old they should have been receiving pensions. Later we learned the Pakistanis preferred old eggs, and often buried them in the ground until they were ready to grow whiskers.

The next few weeks were spent getting acquainted with people and our new surroundings, while we cooled our heels waiting for our house to be readied.

The nights were turning cool now with a breeze contrasting pleasantly with the stifling hot, humid days. We usually spent our evenings under a blanket of stars, propped up in bamboo chairs that overlooked the Arabian Sea, listening to the Viennese Chamber Ensemble which played nostalgic music for the late dinner-dance crowd that flocked to the hotel. The music was perfect for dancing, but since getting my husband onto a dance floor was like getting a cat to have pups, we usually just listened, dreaming of home and speculating about events to come.

If I remember nothing else about Pakistan, I shall always remember her stars. There were millions of them—so brilliant they dazzled us; so near, it seemed as though we could harvest them. The play of their reflections on the rippling water doubled their intensity, and cast a spell of their own on the mysticism of the Middle East. I allowed myself the luxury of succumbing to the spell, only to be snapped out of my reverie each night by Frank, jerking his wrist with a characteristic flip, and saying, "It's late. Gotta go to bed." The strains of the music followed us to our room, and for hours sometimes, I'd listen to the music wafting through the windows as I reflected on the mystery that was Pakistan.

Occasionally, we would hire a taxi to go into town which was about five miles away, and one day, a Greek businessman (one of the hotel's guests) drove us out into the countryside to see his paint factory.

This trip was a real eye-opener. We passed miles of refugee huts, many of them built on swampy, mucky land. Between the road and the huts were native women with piles of camel dung, patting them with their hands in nice, round circles the size of dinner plates, prior to laying them in neat rows to dry. Those that were dry were being loaded onto camel carts and taken to town to be sold as fuel. We noticed a boy about 12 years of age, standing at the back of a truck with his hands spread-eagle across the load of dung, and with his face pressed into it, the truck lumbered down the road!

On a little further, we passed a pond filled with water buffalo relaxing on their bellies in the cool water, while dozens of Pakistani women lined the banks and washed their clothes in the same water. After removing the clothes from the water, they beat them unmercifully with big sticks and then laid them on the railroad tracks to dry. (I wondered where the train was!)

We passed what seemed like an endless procession of women, toting bundles of either dirty or newly washed laundry to and from the pond in baskets upon their heads.

After we left our friend's factory, which was small and neat, he drove us into Karachi's Old City. The vicinity was swarming with people who were sleeping, walking, hawking, shaving, or cooking on the sidewalks while their camels, donkeys and sheep milled nearby. Pedestrians were forced to walk in the street; there was no room on the sidewalks. Donkey carts, camel carts, street cars, rickshaws, bicycles, and two-storied buses lurched crazily in and out of this extraordinary mass of humanity that defied description. Goose wallas, with five or six geese honking in two baskets that were suspended across their shoulders, vied for space with wallas selling everything from fish to straw hats. The sights were incomprehensible; the smells unbelievable. It was a relief to return to our hotel.

One day as we were languishing in our room, Doug burst in breathlessly. "Hey, you guys! Come and see how they wash dishes in this place!"

The girls and I followed him to the rear of the hotel to discover a withered old man with a scraggly white beard, clad only in dirty shorts, squatting cross legged on a table. In between his boney knees was a single pail of putrid water in which he washed the mounds of dishes that surrounded him. After drying the dishes, he stacked them off to his side in piles as high as he was.

As we watched the dishwasher, a bedraggled coolie struggled past us on his way to the kitchen dragging a huge chunk of ice on a gunny sack that was so dirty it was almost black.

"Now I see why you won't let us have ice in our Pakola," Judi and Doug chorused, as we headed for lunch.

We were assigned a permanent table in the dining room, and couldn't help but wonder if "permanent" was a portent of things to come! We were waiting, impatiently now, for the house that was promised us by the FOA Mission, wondering if it would ever materialize. To our chagrin, our table was not in Amir's section, but was instead lorded over by a waiter—stupid, fat and sweaty—whom we dubbed "Rooster" because of his cocky manner and the unusually high plume on his turban.

At lunch one day we watched "Rooster" strutting by as he delivered some chocolate eclairs to a nearby table. We ordered some for dessert.

"Sorry, Mem Sahib. No have today."

"Yes, you do. You just brought some to that other table. Look. Here on the menu it says 'chocolate eclairs'!"

Touching his chin to his portly front, he scrutinized the menu carefully, frowned, then brightening, he stood to full attention and proclaimed with an air of superiority, "Oh, Mem Sahib. That no chocolate! That Number 9."

So it was. Chocolate Eclairs. Number 9 on the menu!

He guarded his tables like a cock in a hen house, and resented any intrusion by any of the other waiters. Undaunted, Amir would rush into "Rooster's" section at every opportunity to feed Joyce and stroke her platinum blonde hair. He was always caught, and always reprimanded, but never failed to try. Like the other waiters, Amir was screamed at by his superiors and many of the hotel guests so often that he was edgy and nearly jumped out of his skin if anyone looked in his direction. We became increasingly fond him, and eventually tried to lure him away from the hotel to be our private bearer when (and if) we ever moved into a house, but he refused because he said he could earn more money at the hotel than in a private home.

"Hotel pay 50 rupees ($16) a month. No much, but I get beegest tip of all bearers," he said proudly.

"But your hours are so long, Amir. Many times we have seen you here until 1:00 or 2:00 o'clock in the morning."

"Yes, hours much long. I work here six years, and never I be to work on time. Hotel take 2 rs. (rupees) every time I late. Last month, hotel take 45 rs. Too bad for me!" he said, shaking his head sadly.

"Why don't you start earlier?"

"Too tired, Mem Sahib. I peddle bicycle to hut. My hut 10 kilometers from here. No get home until two, sometimes three o'clock in the morning. Get maybe three hours sleep. I up at six to peddle my daughter to school before coming to work. Peddle one hour to get here."

We pitied him and the others like him. Life was not easy for them. We were disappointed that he wouldn't be coming with us, but we were wondering if we would ever get a house ourselves. By this time, we had lived out of suitcases in the hotel for five weeks, long enough for us to "lose" all but six tablets of our two-year supply of aspirin, all but three of my hay fever tablets, and the fifth scab from my small pox vaccination that had been infected and feverish since I had been inoculated five months earlier.

We had little to keep us occupied except an insatiable curiosity about the people and their customs. The architecture of the hotel, which was the newest one in Karachi, was ultra-modern. Attractive and clean, it was far superior to anything we had dared to hope for in this hardship post. Situated in the midst of tropical trees and foliage it seemed like a mirage in the desert, for beyond the grounds and the touches of man the surrounding countryside was a barren wasteland of sand.

CHAPTER FOUR

MOHARRAM: DAYS OF MOURNING

We were on an emotional kaleidoscope during the next few weeks—entranced by the novelty of our new experience, shocked by the stark reality of it; homesick, but anxious to get settled in the house that had been promised to us; tired of hotel life, intrigued by hotel life; lonely but busy forming new friends among the hotel guests of many nationalities; puffed out with an arrogant pride because *WE WERE AMERICANS*; deflated like a popped balloon to discover nobody cared.

The hotel proved to be a small United Nations with guests from many countries. We met people from all over the world—Norwegian, Dutch, French and English pilots; businessmen from England, France, Holland, Greece, Scotland; Viennese musicians, and a wonderful couple of Syrian extraction, George and Frieda Thomas, who became close friends of ours.

We were shocked, and taken down a few pegs, when we realized how contemptuous many of them were of

Americans. One of the Norwegian pilots told us, "You Americans try to buy your way all of the time. Why, at the airport in Oslo, I saw a porter throw down a Norwegian's luggage in favor of running over to take an American's bags because he knew he would get a bigger tip."

The British were the bitterest of all. Of course,

England had been shelled and bombed on its own soil; rubble was everywhere, whereas America had escaped the devastation that war brings.

I asked one woman, who was preparing to return to England on home leave, how she felt about going home, and was shocked to hear her say, "How would anybody feel? I'm sure even in America there are better places than this!"

I didn't like hearing this criticism, but realized how lucky we were that global wars had never been fought on our soil. I also realized that envy was at the root of much of their bitterness.

It reached a climax of sorts when an English couple who had been very pointed in their remarks and condescending in their attitude finally outlined the horrors of war that had been experienced on British soil. The woman, who was wearing her bitterness like a badge of honor, said resentfully, "*YOU* don't have bombed out buildings on your soil! *YOU* don't still have a shortage of supplies. Butter and meat are still rationed in England—nylons, too! The best that England possesses is exported to America. "Why, in England the saying is, 'If you want the best that England has to offer, go to America to get it."

With a disdainful sniff, she turned away.

It took a bit of doing, several days' worth, actually, to convince her that it was not our fault, personally, nor the fault of our country that the war was fought on their soil. The discussions continued unabated during many long afternoons. Finally, Frieda and I felt a certain pride when she remarked to us some days later, "You girls have given us an entirely different opinion of America and Americans. Thank you for what you have said."

As time went by it was a wonderful learning experience to make friends with so many foreigners, and we were especially pleased to become friends with several English men and women. I can't imagine any country having so many fun-loving citizens as Britain has, despite the hardships they have endured.

Not only did we meet a lot of interesting people, but we spent a lot of time at the hotel watching the natives tackle their jobs. We were especially amused to watch the sweepers scoot around on their haunches, like spiders, as they swept the floors with their feathery brooms.

"Look at that man washing the steps," Judi said, pointing to a sweeper dressed in what looked like white (or what used to be white) diapers. A naked boy, about four years old, was clinging precariously onto his shoulders, as the sweeper navigated the stairs with the typical short-handled broom and a bucket of water. He splashed water onto the steps, then brushed them with the broom that was no more than three feet long with feathery-type branches that were perfect for mopping up the water and sweeping up the fine dust and sand that powdered everything they touched.

We frequently went for walks when the evenings cooled a bit, oftentimes coming upon men (never women) in trancelike prayers, always facing Mecca, which was the birthplace of their prophet, Mohammed. One day I marveled at the extraordinary balance of a Muslim kneeling on a foot-wide railing of a little bridge as he prayed to Allah! Another evening by chance we stumbled upon about five hotel employees lined up on a special platform alongside the hotel. They stood with folded arms on their prayer mats in intense concentration, their shoes lined up neatly behind them. With closed eyes, they stood there for several seconds, and then they bowed down rhythmically, kneeled in unison, and touched their foreheads to their prayer mats. As though on cue, they all rose, and repeated their actions for minutes on end. Their religion demanded that they perform this ritual five times a day—at sunrise, sunset and three times in between.

The Muslim religion was so forceful that it dictated every action; more than a religion, it was a way of life. It was so powerful, that their religion was largely responsible for the Pakistanis breaking away from Hindu India to form their own country in 1947.

The depth of their religion was emphasized sharply one afternoon about two weeks after our arrival. Our friend, George Thomas, knocked on our hotel door.

"Frank, I've made arrangements for the two of us to witness an all night ritual by some religious fanatics tonight. Do you want to go?

"What is it all about?" Frank asked.

"Tomorrow is the seventh day of the Moharram mourning period. Tonight is the night they beat themselves with swords, knives and chains to atone for the murder of Mohammed's grandson. Westerners are usually not allowed to see this ceremony, but I have a Pakistani friend who said if we would dress in old clothes and be as inconspicuous as possible, he would take us to this orgy. Sorry," he added, looking sternly at his wife, Frieda, and me. "women are never allowed to watch these rites."

Frank, George and his friend, Col. Asghar, arose at the break of dawn to witness the event. Begum (Mrs.) Asghar joined Frieda and me later to wait for the men as they stole away to view the vicarious suffering of the devout.

Later, Frank said the ritual began with 200 or 300 men gathered in a circle at the edge of town. "They were all stripped to the waist, wearing only lungis [skirts men wore that were made of five yards of material that they wound around their waists]. Many of them had tucked the material between their legs, making a pair of shorts.

"Someone began chanting, and then others joined in. Pretty soon they were all chanting and swaying in a sort of rhythmic dance, hopping to the left, then hopping to the right. While they were doing this, they began hitting themselves on their own backs with swords, knives or chains, slowly at first, then faster and faster and faster until after awhile they were screaming and beating themselves hysterically in a wild frenzy. They seemed to have mesmerized themselves. Their chants reached a wild, weird, frenzied crescendo as they whirled, hitting themselves faster and faster; harder and harder. They were like maniacs. Some of them continued beating themselves until they dropped. One man died. The rest were covered with blood. It was horrible!"

"What is the significance of this ritual?" I asked.

"They feel they are commemorating the martyrdom of Hussain, the grandson of the prophet. He and his entire family were ambushed in the desert and kept without food and water for three days before being killed by a mob over 1,300 years ago.

"This is one reason it is dangerous for foreigners to witness this ritual. They are lashing out at the 'enemies' who killed Hussain, and when they get in that hysterical trance, there's no telling when they might lash out at outsiders."

"While we were waiting, Begum Asghar told us a lot about the mourning period, but she didn't mention anything about what you have just seen," I said.

"What did she say?"

"She said when there is a 'Moharram moon' [a sliver of a new moon], the faithful begin each day by reading descriptive poems which dramatize the events that are said to have happened each day so long ago.

"The tragedy has been taken out of the realm of purely religious devotion for the family and put into an extremely high-level climax that is reached when they relive the deaths of the prophet's grandson and his family. She said the poems are beautiful and have been made to live throughout the centuries by vivid, poignant examples of religious genius that give the incidents elements of tragic drama.

"Then she began relating some of the rituals that took place during Moharram.

"On the seventh day of mourning, believers perform the mock fight and commemorate the betrothal of Quassim with Kurbra, Imam Husain's daughter; and on the ninth, the waiting of doom; and the tenth morning, the holocaust. On the ninth night and tenth afternoon, they march in a huge procession carrying elaborate tazias, replicas of tombs that were constructed by different guilds. For example, the tazias of malis [gardeners] were made of green grass and leaves; tazias of banglemakers were made entirely of bangles; tazias of cotton weavers were made of cotton, and so on. The tazias were huge; some of them appeared to be from seven to eight feet tall or taller and were carried on the shoulders of men to the accompaniment of martial music, lighted torches, banners and shields. The marchers walked right into the river and 'drowned' the evil spirits by submerging the tazias completely in the murky water. On the eleventh day, they commemorated the looting of the tents and taking of prisoners; on the twelfth, the weary trudged to Damascus; and on the thirteenth, they commemorated the burying of the dead."

Moharram (Days of Mourning) is the only festival in which Muslims use symbolic representations, a custom derived from association with India and Persia. At intervals of a few days, the various incidents that were said to have taken place during the period of imprisonment were celebrated, and so it went until the fortieth day when they celebrated the return to Medina.

During Moharram women dressed in black, but since jewelry was not allowed to be worn at this time, they were adept at combining jewels, sequins, and a variety of trims on the black fabric to brighten it.

"Special food prepared for Moharram was 'khhichra,' which contained five or seven different kinds of grain and meat cooked together. The mixture simmered all night. It was always cooked in large quantities because it, and sweetened iced drinks, were customarily given to the poor on the seventh and the tenth days of Moharram."

Frank, still visibly shaken by having witnessed the wild, hysterical, beatings returned to the discussion of the ritual that had just taken place.

"Col. Asghar said that the men at the orgy last night were all from the same sect," he said.

"Yes," Frieda countered. "Mrs. Asghar said the Shiites, from the Shia sect, are the most devout, and are the strictest about observing this ritual.

She said some of the fanatics observe forty days of mourning, although most of them observe only thirteen days. During the mourning period, the faithful aren't allowed to marry, have any sexual activity, give parties, chew beetle nut, or do anything frivolous during this time."

Thousands of people participated in the huge Moharram Day parade. The following year we (women and men) were allowed to watch the frenzied dances and the procession from the roof of the FOA building. We took movies of the entire event, and the multitudes of onlookers that swarmed into the streets after the parade. The gyrating crowd in the street below, a solid mass of humanity as far as we could see, was so frenzied that we became dizzy watching them.

During the parade, two planes collided above our heads, spilling fuel over some of the onlookers that were with us on the roof of the FOA building. Although I had my camera, I stupidly did not photograph the incident. The report about the collision was on the front page of the *Dawn Newspaper* that evening. The next day, there was a retraction saying there absolutely had not been a collision! Go figure!

Three days later, which was the tenth day of mourning, we set out with George and Frieda to witness the end of the boisterous, frenzied parade. To the accompaniment of martial music, lighted torches, banners and shields, thousands of participants carried replicas of tombs on their shoulders to the water's edge. The replicas were ornate and beautifully detailed, usually fashioned from bamboo and paper, but some were of grass and leaves, and one, we noticed, was of bangles.

"What are they going to do with them?" Judi said, transfixed as they approached the river banks.

"They are going to drown the evil spirits," Frieda said. "Look."

As she spoke, the onlookers moved aside as though on cue, and the marchers, chanting and screaming, waded out into the polluted water, pushing the intricately designed tombs into the water until they were completely submerged. Then, with triumphant shouts, they emerged from the water amid cheers from their friends, and gaily danced away. The parade had ended, and so for most purposes, had the period of mourning. Until next year.

CHAPTER FIVE

THE "CRAZY HOUSE"

The days were stifling hot during the last two weeks of October. I understood why few of the European women had sun tans. It was simply too hot to sun bathe.

When we arrived in Karachi on September 18, we were told that our house was completed and all they had to do was clean it up and move the furniture in. The government had been paying $400 a month for a period of time to hold the house, and we were coughing up $300 per month for hotel accommodations and nothing seemed to be happening! But after witnessing the Moharram Day parade, we walked thoughtfully back to our hotel, evaluating without judgment the events of the last few days. As we approached the lobby of the Beach Luxury Hotel, one of Frank's counterparts rushed out to meet us.

"We have a house for you. You can move in next week. You have been assigned the Crazy House!"

"The what?"

"The Crazy House!"

We had been offered a house called The Crazy House which infuriated Frank until Forrest drove us out to see it. Our first impression of the Crazy House was that it was an ultra modern, cement mansion, towering well back inside a compound wall. When Forrest honked, a chowkidar (guard) hurried out to swing open the massive wrought iron gate. We eased our way into the compound, past a guest house built above three garages, and inched to a stop in front of some steps that led to, of all things, the *back* door. Later we dropped in for a chat with the occupant of the guest house, a Miss Bateman, who proved to be the nurse who helped Lowell Thomas escape from Tibet.

Further examination revealed why our new home was called the *crazy* house. It was indeed *crazy,* but magnificent!

Designed by a Pakistani woman, which was in itself unheard of in a country where women were just beginning to shed their veils, the house was as unusual as the designer herself. The back door was in front; the front door was in back, overlooking an enormous yard. It was constructed on several different levels with 47 steps from the lower level to the "penthouse" (walled in roof). The stairs were circular with a graceful slope that not only made them easier to climb, but added to the beauty of the interior. Counting the screened-in porch, a large play room and a walk-in fruit room (storage room) there were 14 rooms in our portion of the Crazy House. Most of the better homes in Karachi were designed as two-family dwellings, and this was no exception. We were assigned two-thirds of the house, and the remaining third was already occupied by an American family.

As we entered the back door of our part of the mansion, we found ourselves in a large circular entrance hall, with a circular wall facing the door, and a circular outside wall encased in glass brick, overlooking the compound from which we had entered. Beyond the entrance hall, we observed an enormous living room and an adjoining giant-sized dining room. The outer wall of the dining room featured a circular glassed-in wall that overlooked the large front yard (which was in back).

Down about 10 stairs from the dining room were two kitchens and a breakfast room; two steps further down was the fruit room, a storage room, which we were soon to dub the "swimming pool" because it was built below ground level and seeped three gallons of salt water each week through its walls. (We later learned that trying to solve the seepage problem in that room was the reason for the delay in moving us into the house.)

The kitchens, built for servants, were small and inconvenient, without cupboards or built-ins of any sort. Since Pakistanis squat to do almost everything, the hot water faucets were installed a foot above the floor, with a drain in the floor. One of the kitchens had a built-in charcoal stove, which loosely resembled an American barbecue grill. We later installed our kerosene stove (with its prized oven) in this room.

The second kitchen had a higher faucet, and a sink, both hip high. Here the cook had his work table and pantry. On the same level was the breakfast room, and down two steps, the "swimming pool". My favorite room in the whole house was the breakfast room, a sunny room with its walls of various-sized stones, some were the size of large cantaloupes. This room was built partially underground. On the outside wall of this room was our water tank, which held the drinking water. Later, our two rabbits and one parrot were housed below the water tank. Before long, this area also sheltered Mem Sahib, our dachshund pup, and two more parrots.

Going back to the entrance hall level inside, we began climbing the spiral staircase to the first landing, which exited into a large master bedroom and private bath. Positioned in the center of one wall was an armoire—a piece of furniture about seven feet high and five feet wide to be used to store clothes since there were no built-in closets.

Continuing our circular climb, we emerged onto the next level, which held two more large bedrooms with circular outer walls. A screened-in sun porch encircled and connected the bedrooms, which had individual armoires in each. In the hallway as we approached the second bedroom was a 30-foot stretch of built-in cupboards designed for storage. This feature was very rare in Pakistani architecture, which seldom included closets in the building plans. Each bedroom had its own bathroom, and in Doug's bathroom (the last bathroom on the top level of the house), was a 15-gallon water tank—the only water tank in the whole house! The kitchens were on the bottom levels without any hot water unless we boiled it. Doug's bathroom became home for our washing machine. Hot water for dishes had to be boiled 47 steps below on the stove.

Hot water for bathing was unimportant because the mean average temperature in Karachi was 92 degrees. The "usual" temperature, it seemed to me, was 107 degrees. This meant the water in the outdoor water tank was heated by the "automatic solar" method, which was usually comfortable. If not comfortable, it was usually wet, unless the water tank went dry, which happened.

As the moving day approached, we made frequent trips by taxi to the house. Whenever we asked taxi drivers to go to 34 D Drigh Road, we received a blank stare; no sign of comprehending. If we said, "Crazy House," they jumped to attention and whizzed us straight there! Everyone in town knew the Crazy House, and before long, we were to wish we had never heard of it.

The Crazy House was located 10 miles outside the Karachi City limits. We actually felt stranded because our only neighbors had private homes within high compound walls, sealed in by heavy iron gates (as did ours). Our chowkidar stood guard on the grounds all night. We were told there were many thieves in Karachi who would kill for less than $50 without batting an eye.

Finally, on October 30, six weeks after our arrival, we moved into the house. Our household goods had not yet arrived, so Frank bought four sheets, a few towels, two pots and a frying pan, and the Embassy loaned us a small oven, dishes, silverware and glasses. Each of the bedrooms had three-quarter-size beds. We put one sheet on each of three beds (Joyce and Judi shared a bed), and used the fourth one as a tablecloth. The weather had warmed up again after the brief September respite from the heat due to the monsoon haze, and we didn't need covers over us at night, although it was getting a little cool in the mornings.

Camping in style, I baked a two-pound canned ham and boiled some carrots and potatoes for our first dinner in our new house. I had planned to bake the potatoes, but there wasn't room for both ham and potatoes in the 12-inch square oven that the State Department furnished.

As soon as we moved in, we set about getting the kinks out of the place. The Pakistanis had good ideas about construction, we discovered, but knew very little about how to finish things properly. Wiring was left outside of the plaster, bathtubs were encased in tile, but a ½-inch space was left between the tub and the wall. Water, instead of running down pipes, drained onto the floors in all three bathrooms. Toilets flushed only when they wanted to, which wasn't often. Oh, well, we figured, at least we had inside plumbing.

To think it would soon be Halloween in the States, and I was still wearing sun-backed dresses! Luckily all of the rooms in the Crazy House had large circulating fans in the ceilings, and all of the floors were of terrazzo tile, except the kitchens, which had cement floors.

On October 30, we received our third refrigerator from the government. The first one they installed refused to run; the second one ran but didn't keep the food cold. Finally we hit the jackpot. They installed a brand new Crosley Shelvador—the kind I had always wanted. I was ecstatic!

Halloween came and went; by now, it was early November, and we had three durzees (tailors) working at the house all day making our draperies. Removing their shoes, they put them neatly against the wall. Then, one of the men brought in the strangest looking portable Singer sewing machine that I had ever seen. It had no table and no legs. One of the durzees placed the sewing machine on the floor, sat cross legged in front of it, and proceeded to sew the sill-length drapes by working the wheel swiftly with his right hand. He held the material between his toes and guided the fabric with his left hand. The second man did the cutting and the hanging, and the third man sewed rings at the top of the drapes. The house looked fabulous when they had finished, and we no longer felt as though we were living in a fishbowl.

Our household goods eventually arrived on December fifth. After having lived out of suitcases for three months, one day and about 17 hours, it was a big relief. Frank stayed home from work and opened the seven large wooden crates himself rather than wait for the coolies to get around to it. Then we worked for one whole week putting 10,000 lbs. of "stuff "away!

Living in Karachi was more pleasant now that we had a few conveniences and I began cooking and baking up a storm. The kerosene stove that I had purchased was a pure delight. The oven baked beautifully, better than our Tappan did at home. I baked fabulous rolls and pies, rolling out the dough with a wine bottle until I finally found and unpacked the rolling pin that we had shipped. Soon, I was baking nine loaves of bread every other day. We could buy fairly good bread on the market for 35 cents a loaf, but frequently there were unbaked hunks of yeast, or something doughy, distributed here and there throughout the loaves, which was unappetizing to say the least.

While we were waiting for our bearer, we hired a dhobi (laundryman) who, I soon learned the hard way, showed up when he wanted to, and didn't the rest of the time. Early on, I soaked the white clothes in Clorox in anticipation of his visit. When the dhobi didn't show up, I proceeded to wash the clothes myself. In Pakistan, that was an undertaking! To begin with, our hot water heater, which we had had for three weeks, was not yet connected. So the hamal carried hot water up all of the steps from the kitchen to Doug's bathroom to do the wash, and rinsed the laundry in Doug's bathtub. This wasn't too bad, except the wringer didn't fit over the tub far enough, so most of the water ran out on the floor. There was so much water on the floor by the time I finished washing that I decided I might as well empty it all into the floor drain, not realizing that the floor sloped *away* from the drain. There the water was, ankle deep. I took off my shoes and tried to detour the water, and *YIKES*!—almost got electrocuted trying to get the machine unplugged!

A few days later, we got the water heater connected, but the water wouldn't run out of the pipes. It seems that when they built the house, they used two sizes of pipes, causing a bottleneck somewhere, which shut off the water.

Privacy was nonexistent. I began to get used to a constant stream of motley men coming in and out of the house and yard. For the past week, a team of malis had been digging out the yard to a depth of two feet with pick axes, preparatory to putting in top soil. We were told the soil had to be removed because it was solid clay and the ground was so salty nothing would grow in it. We wanted the malis to do a nice job of landscaping so, in addition to planting flowers, we asked them to plant a lot of banana trees for shade, but they resisted. "No, Ma'am," one of them said. "They take too long to grow."

"How long would they take?"

"It would take nine months for them to get four feet high!" was the response.

CHAPTER SIX

SO MUCH POVERTY; SO MUCH WEALTH

Pakistan was a contradiction in terms. We had never seen so much wealth, and so much poverty; so many mansions, so many slums. The newly-formed country had been inundated with refugees who had fled from India after Partition in 1947. Muslims had fled from India into Pakistan; Hindus from Pakistan into India, 14 million in all. In 1953, we learned that 1.5 million of them—between 48% and 52% of Karachi's population—were living in refugee camps that had been erected haphazardly on vacant land throughout the city without sanitary facilities of any sort. Instead, "benjou" ditches ran alongside the roads carrying human waste in all of the camps. The smell was horrible. Beggars were everywhere. Children and adults were oftentimes barefoot, summer and winter. We felt guilty having more than they had; we thanked God that we *did have* more than they had!

Most of the refugees existed with mud floors and little or no furniture. Oftentimes, they lived, cooked and slept in one tiny room in huts that were honeycombed throughout the fields. Here they lived with large families, their camels, goats, fat-tailed sheep, and dogs. A hole in the dirt floor served as a toilet; a pit in another corner served as a stove; women squatted outside of the huts, grinding spices and making chappatis by flipping the dough back and forth between their hands. When the chappatis were thin enough, they tossed them onto a heated stone to cook. The chappatis were delicious! Surprisingly, the slums lacked the debris that our slums have. The clay floors were swept clean several times a day, and the occupants were too poor to even have junk around their places. It seemed to us that most of the working class people were refugees, pitiful dregs of a society that found it was to its advantage to keep locals poor and illiterate. As a result, the refugees received little or no help from their own people.

It didn't take the Pakistanis long to catch on to the American system, however. Prices increased threefold. Everything on the local market was very expensive, two to three times the price of the same goods in the States, which irritated the local population. Servants preferred working for Americans rather than for their own people because our people were said to be kinder to them, and we paid them higher salaries.

Typical salaries in 1953 for servants (which varied depending on the size of the residence, the size of the family, and general requirements) were:

Bearer (head servant):	carried out the duties of both valet and butler, including interpreting; received Rs. (rupees) 75 to 180 ($23 to $60) per month.
Cook:	(managed kitchen, cooked and bought foodstuffs): Wage scale same as bearer; cook/bearer received higher salary, depending on competence.
Hamal (second servant):	assisted in serving at the table, did the dusting, washed dishes, and did general work; Rs. 40 to 60 ($13 to $18) per month.
Dhobi (laundryman):	did the personal and household laundry (excluding dry cleaning) for Rs.30 ($9) per month, more if they worked in the home. Most of them did not work on the premises, but we trained ours to use the washing machine and electric iron (for which they charged us more!).

	They received about Rs.40 to 60 ($13 to $18) per month.
Sweeper (janitor):	(next to the lowest class, just above coolies cleaned the floors and the bathrooms and performed all of the work others refused to do, such as emptying the garbage, and cleaning up after the dog in the yard. Salary unknown, but less than other servants.
Coolie (lowest class):	Never used in American homes. Did dirtiest, hardest jobs. Salary unknown.
Mali (gardener):	did the work that gardeners do best for a monthly salary of Rs.55 to 70 ($18 to $22.75).
Chowkidar (guard):	protected the house and compound, particularly at night, for Rs.40 to 60 ($13 to $18) per month. Salary paid by U.S. government.

There were also servants such as amahs and chauffeurs which we did not use at our house. We started out with a bearer (and without a cook), hamal, dhobi, sweeper and mali. I soon changed my mind, and before long we hired a cook/bearer.

Life of Riley? Not quite! While having servants enabled us to participate in more activities, and there was a heavy social schedule, they created a lot of problems. Servants were not a luxury but a necessity when it came to dealing with the language, shopping, the different culture, customs, religion and climate. We soon learned we were responsible not only for our servants, but by extension, their families. Most of them had large families, and if one of them became ill or had serious problems, chances are we would be asked to help.

If doing the laundry was difficult, and banana trees took too long to grow, it was an equal challenge to buy things at the market (bazaar). Shopping in the bazaar was difficult not only because of the language problem, but because it was customary to bargain for everything. We were told the surest way to bargain was to 1) drop the asking price by half and 2) come up half way of the dropped price. For example, if the asking price was 8 rupees, you offered the walla 4 rs. and settled for 6 rs. We were told that if we started to walk away when the walla didn't accept the 6rs. offer he would then run after you. I spent more than three years in Karachi and never once did a walla run after me!

Prices for most foodstuffs that were locally grown were inexpensive. Prawns, lobster and other seafood were marvelous, and were from 8 annas (15 cents) to one rupee (33 cents) a pound. Almost all cuts of meat were from about 12 annas to1/rs. per lb., including T-bone steaks and sirloin, but don't let that fool you. The meat was usually tough. Adolph's meat tenderizer was a must in a Karachi kitchen. Fruit was plentiful and cheap in season. At a peak season, apples were about $1 per lb., but bananas, were $2.49/lb. The import tax tripled the cost of many imported products. For example, I paid 2 rs., 12 annas (90 cents) for a can of cornstarch that was the size of a salt box.

Clothing was way out of reason because most cloth was imported. However, to have garments made (if you had the material) was very small since labor was so cheap. I had two formals made. One cost $5.00 for workmanship; the other $7.00. That didn't include the cost of replacing the thread that was stolen.

In the main part of Karachi, there were shops that resembled some of our smaller shops at home. Most shops were rickety, messy booths, stacked high with merchandise of every description. Everything was sold in the open. Flies covered foodstuffs like blankets. When disturbed, the black "blanket" rose and flew away in one fell swoop, revealing a dish of yellow corn or some other foodstuff underneath. Food and goods were almost always unwrapped, except for bread, which the wallas wrapped in newspapers before tossing the loaves into our basket. If we wanted meat or fish, they hacked off a hunk, and threw it on top of whatever else was in our basket; seafood was handed to us loose and sometimes alive, and fruit and vegetables were handed to us loose. On a good note, tropical fruit—mangoes, watermelon, pineapple and papaya—were delicious, plentiful and inexpensive.

Even though I always got a little nauseated when I went to the bazaar, I couldn't help but be intrigued (and depressed). Here, primitive was mixed with modern. Hundreds of natives walked on the streets and sidewalks, jammed together like shoppers at a Macy's sale, dodging cars, camel carts, donkey carts, man-pulled carts, tongas (horse-drawn carriages), rickshas, herds of buffalo, goats, sheep and donkeys. Oftentimes men were seen trotting down the street hauling heavy loads on their backs, and countless women shuffled along toting loads of everything imaginable on their heads. Bazaar shopping was depressing, for many reasons, but one was because the wallas were painfully frank. For example, I decided one day to buy a pair of sandals. The procedure was to sit in front of the shoe walla, who was squatting on the ground. He would then draw the outline of his customer's foot on a piece of paper. He drew my foot. The drawing almost ran off the page. He looked up at me horrified, saying, "Mem Sahib, never I see feet beeg like theez before!"

It was intriguing to watch craftsmen making by hand all sorts of things such as Persian rugs. We went to a small shop where they made and sold exquisite Persian rugs—the real McCoy—and were they gorgeous! The one I coveted was 4500 rupees or $1,500 for a 4' x 6' size. Frank preferred one that was a mere $1,000 for the same size.

Next we watched two fellows weaving rugs in an alley booth that was only as large as the space they needed for sitting. They had what appeared to be hundreds of colored yarns hanging from the makeshift ceiling. Without missing a beat, they grabbed the color thread that they needed in their left hand, tied a knot and cut it with a knife held in the right hand. All so fast you had to scrutinize their actions carefully in order to see what they were doing. They sat cross-legged all day long on a little bench that was only big enough for the two of them, occasionally singing out directions to each other in a native chant, or stopping momentarily to study a drawing that was made to scale and tacked to the wall of their stall. They were able to make one-half inch of a four foot-wide carpet a day, and could complete a 4'x6' carpet in about nine months!

It didn't matter if you were looking at socks, bras, pants, or false teeth, signs galore were saying "One size fits all." Things were sold, bought and eaten on the sidewalks. Camels were tied to trees while masters tended to their business. Men, private parts shielded from view by baggy shalwar pants, were squatting with their backs turned as they urinated against the fences. Streets were teeming with men and women carrying loads of every description on their heads; vendors were pulling at our arms as they hawked their wares, but the payoff came when a boy about Doug's age approached us carrying two fat, white geese. "Geese, Sahib? Geese, Sahib?" It was a reminder that all poultry was sold alive and killed at home. If we had purchased them, couldn't you picture us carrying two live geese around as we shopped?

One of the highlights of our stay in Pakistan was the state visit by then Vice President Richard M. Nixon and Mrs. Nixon on December 6. 1953. Americans turned out en masse; children, all 40 or so of them, were dismissed from school for the day. The entire diplomatic corps—all military officers and other personnel in dress uniforms designating their rank or position, government and private officials—in short, the entire American community was in attendance, as were dignitaries from foreign embassies who were dressed in their native costumes.

Judi was thrilled to have been one of two students to have had her name drawn from a hat to greet Pat Nixon upon her arrival at the airport. Vice President Nixon reviewed the Pakistan Honor guard, bagpipes played, and Judi and six-year-old Laurie Duncan presented Mrs. Nixon with a card and a lovely floral bouquet. Doug and Judi both shook hands with the Nixons, and Judi refused to let her hand touch anything else for a full three hours afterwards. There were an estimated 1,000 people in the receiving line and the Nixons remained gracious throughout. We thought they were marvelous ambassadors of goodwill for the United States.

CHAPTER SEVEN

SHAFI FIRED; AZIZ HIRED

We were pleasantly surprised one night when Shafi, our bearer, said he would cook dinner for us as a "thank-you" for our kindness to him. He cooked chapattis (unleavened bread much like tortillas) and curry. The food was delicious! Usually people wouldn't eat any servant's food, especially when they prepared it in their own quarters as he did, because their standards of cleanliness are seldom in keeping with ours. However, we had no reason to be concerned about food that Shafi prepared because he was meticulously clean. Our only problem was a feeling of regret that he would be so kind to us when we were so unhappy with him.

Our first Christmas in Karachi, a simple one, was rapidly approaching. I bought a little artificial tree and some green and orange (couldn't find red) crepe paper to decorate it. We had only a few gifts for the children because Santa Claus was late in delivery. I knew I would be a mess if I didn't keep busy so I baked cookies by the dozens three or four days before Christmas, made rolls, baked three cherry pies, and stuffed and baked two geese and all of the trimmings for our 15 Christmas dinner guests. I couldn't help thinking about the Christmas Eves in Denver when I invariably would be sewing final stitches on clothes or doll clothes until two or three in the morning only to be awakened around 4 a.m. by the children, who had discovered that Santa Claus had arrived. There would be none of that in Karachi. Sears Roebuck was Santa Claus, and he had not arrived.

In a weak moment, I had invited 52 guests to an Open House the Sunday after Christmas. I shuddered at the thought because our new bearer, the honest one from Kashmir, was now working for us. Shafi may have been honest, but he was slower than molasses and twice as sticky. He was presentable in appearance, looked more Italian than Mid-Eastern, was of middle age and medium height and had a long, black handlebar mustache through which he wheezed when he talked.

Shafi brought along his own assistant, a grizzly-looking fellow who was tall and barefooted with henna-dyed hair and beard, beetle-juice-stained teeth, dark gray shirt, and full gray shalwar pants. Even though the temperature was 92 degrees, his "ensemble" was topped with a heavy wool sweater and wool stocking cap. We were decidedly not impressed with the way Abdullah looked, but reluctantly gave Shafi and his judgment the benefit of the doubt. We hired Abdullah, too.

For our Open House, I had prepared fancy little canapés and hors d'oeuvres, baked a pound cake to go with the cookies that I had baked earlier and to compensate for Shafi's deficiencies, hired two additional bearers to help serve. The party couldn't have been more successful, but it pointed out more clearly than ever how inefficient our servant was. As an aside, we were pleased to note that our living room could have easily held another 50 people (standing), and the yard could easily have held 600 guests.

To complicate matters, I had promised Judi she could have a dinner party the preceding night. Judi and Linda Christie, her best friend, planned to cook it themselves for 16 invitees. A couple of nights before their party, we found ourselves eating dinner with two live chickens squawking and running excitedly with flapping wings, underneath our dining room table. Seems Shafi had purchased the chickens for Judi's party, and just turned them loose downstairs until he could find a Christian cook to kill them. Neither Shafi nor Abdullah could "use the axe on them" Shafi said, because they were devout Muslims and it was against their religion.

"We have to pray to god, blow on knife and cut throats so no heads come off" in order to have their 'actions' sanctioned," he explained.

Saturday arrived and dinner preparations were underway by the two girls. It was 6:15 p.m. and Linda was saying, "If the potatoes are done, we can fix 'em anyway we want to and everything will be 'purrrrfect'! I think if we take a shower, it will be quicker than a bath, don't you? Oh, well, maybe a bath will be better."

"I don't care as long as I get wet and get dry again, that's all that matters," Judi snapped.

"Oh, doesn't the table look neat? Everything's turning out just super. I've never had so much fun since I've been in Karachi," Linda gushed, twirling around the kitchen. "I like this kitchen. I like this house!"

Judi and Linda had prepared the chicken, were boiling potatoes and had put the biscuits in the oven. Judi disappeared to fill the bath tubs with water, but soon returned in an agitated state.

"The showers aren't working, and I can't fill both tubs. If I turn on mine, the water won't run into the other tub. We'll just have to take turns."

Judi, who was nursing a cut finger, moaned, "Mother, the stove won't light and I can't find the plug to plug in the roaster."

"Something tells me this is going to be hilarious," Linda laughed.

"Hilarious, nothing," Judi spat. "It's not funny!"

"Come on, Judi, we knew this was going to be awful! We looked forward to it being awful!"

"The potatoes don't know how to mash—they're so soft and squishy."

"Now, see you—"

"Just mash 'em! I don't care how!" Judi said, angrily. "Don't anybody trip on the cord—. *Yikes! The biscuits!"* she screamed. They had been forgotten in the rush of things. She dashed to the oven and rescued them just before they turned to charcoal. "Oooh, I'll never have time for a bath," Judi wailed. It was 6:37. The guests would arrive in twenty minutes.

To everyone's surprise, the evening was a success even though one of the boys brought his two-year-old brother. The dinner, consisting of biscuits, creamed chicken, corn croquettes, mashed potatoes, fruit Jello, chocolate cake and grape juice, was really good, especially for a first attempt by the 12-year-olds.

An unexpected guest was a boy who was just passing through Karachi to another post. It turned out all right, though, because he was *cute* and all of the girls were happy. After dinner, they square danced, than after much reluctance on the part of the boys, the girls succeeded in getting them to do a little social dancing. Since the boys were too shy to ask them to dance, they drew names for partners. Judi drew the new boy's name—too bad he was just passing through. He was a *winner!*

At 8:30 the next morning, our neighbor dropped in and was soon followed by three other visitors—one by one. By noon three of them had left but my neighbor, who was suffering from severe depression, stayed on. I finally invited her to have lunch with me, and she spent the next couple of hours telling me about her shock treatments and how she was scheduled to have eight additional ones.

It was hard to put our fingers on why life was so frustrating in Karachi when we were having so many fascinating experiences. During the time we were there, we heard that two American women had been sent home in straight jackets. In my case, when I reached the point that I thought I couldn't stand it another minute, it became funny. That saved the day.

Karachi had the reputation for being the worst hardship post from the standpoint of people being unable to tolerate their foreign assignment. You couldn't possibly understand how difficult it was to manage a household with people working for you whom you could not easily understand, who couldn't understand you, who had different customs, and when you would ask them to do a certain job, would invariably say, "No, Mem Sahib, the 'Book' (Koran) say no."

On January six, three and one-half months after our arrival, our car was finally uncrated. What a relief that was. We felt as though we had been liberated! The brand new Chevrolet sported a right hand drive, white sidewalls, tinted glass, and a cream and green paint job. We could finally drive around Karachi and photograph some of the fascinating scenes we had been seeing. We were confident that we could master the right hand drive, and learn how to drive on the left side of the roads, but were aghast at the price of petrol (gasoline) at $1.09 an imperial gallon (five quarts). I was told that officials wanted to change traffic to the right side of the street, but couldn't do so because camels, the main "trucking" means, had been trained to walk on the left side. That was an important factor, because most "trucking" was done by camel carts at night. The drivers often fall asleep, but the camels kept plugging right along, and rarely went on the wrong side of the road.

Later, they tried to install a traffic light, but had to take it out because they couldn't teach the camels to stop at red lights.

The second day we had the car, I drove downtown and into the Bori Bazaar district which was a solid mass of humanity, bicycles, rickshas, camel and donkey carts. I managed to escape with nary an incident, with one exception—I barely touched a bicycle with the car. I guess the bicyclist wasn't concerned, because neither of us stopped. I figured hitting anything short of a camel was pretty good.

A few weeks later, I was slowly backing out of our compound when a coolie-type woman came running down the street and threw herself under my car! Luckily, I was going so slow that I was able to stop before the wheel touched her. Our hamal quickly caught her and called the authorities. She tearfully explained that she needed money and thought she could get it by pretending to be injured!

Coolies were slowly making progress in the yard. They had finally cleared out the salty clay to a depth of two feet, and began filling in our back (sorry—the front) yard with cinders at the rate of one donkey cart of cinders every other day. Once the cinders were in place, they topped them with top soil, preparatory to planting the grass *one blade at a time,* because, the gardeners explained, grass seeds would not grow in Karachi's soil!

It was shocking to observe the coolies push, pull, hit and beat their little donkeys. The donkeys were about half the size of our donkeys, and the coolies were so mean to them that we could hardly stand it. I witnessed one occasion when the donkey's load was so heavy that he collapsed from the weight only to be beaten unmercifully by his driver to try to force him to stand.

Winter had set in, and now on January 7, we were suddenly cold! Our house, which was made of cement with 12-foot high ceilings, had no furnaces or fireplaces, and the chill was a penetrating, damp cold. It had been as warm as the low 70's during the daytime in the sun, but after dark it was a different story. One night, it got down to 49 degrees and four people died of pneumonia in a refugee camp two miles from our house. They had contracted the disease partly because of the cold weather, but also because of poor living conditions in their huts which were built from bamboo, mud, tin, straw, rags or newspapers. For the past three days it had been raining, and the natives were miserable. They were oftentimes barefoot, wrapped in blankets and shaking with teeth chattering as they braved the elements. We were lucky, though, because Frank was able to borrow a small heater from the Embassy. It wasn't a whole lot of help in our cavernous rooms, but it was something to huddle around in the smallest room we could find. I wished the poor natives could have shared it with us.

We fired our first dhobi because of dishonesty and poor work, and hired a new dhobi who was absolutely marvelous. He washed and ironed much better than I could. He had never seen a washing machine before and was so in awe of it that he brought his 11-year-old daughter over to see it.

I wondered what the catch would be because this dhobi seemed to be too good to be true. I soon learned that he wanted to move his wife and five children into our garage! There already were 10 children in our compound—our three, our neighbor's two and their servant's five.

I left the decision up to Frank (who was not in favor) but I felt so sorry for the dhobi. He was pathetically poor, and lived in a refugee camp five miles from our compound. It had poured down rain for the past few days and the ground was flooded with lakes of water. My dhobi walked to and from his hut barefooted because he didn't own a bicycle or a pair of shoes. I asked him if he needed money (which he did) so I advanced him a few weeks' pay. The next day he came to work grinning from ear to ear with a new pair of tennis shoes on his feet, proud as a peacock.

He, and thousands of others, had been literally rained out of their huts. Everything they owned got soaking wet and most of them were sick with colds or pneumonia. The rains, heavier than usual, had taken their toll. Three times during the past month, there had been torrential rains, rains that were said to be the first in recorded history, outside of monsoons, to have devastated the area and its people so badly. The ground was a solid mass of lakes. It was so clay-like that the water seemed to evaporate rather than drain. No one had been prepared for such rainfall. None of the streets had drains and everything was a mess. I noticed one of the main streets downtown was waist deep in water. One boy was taking a bath in it; another was washing his bicycle; a man was trying to pull his donkey and cart through it, while several children were having the time of their lives splashing around in it.

One day, we saw a group of men carrying a wooden box in the rain toward the cemetery. Draped over the box, which was more like a board with a frame around it, was a dark cloth that partially covered a body swathed in white, like a mummy. At the cemetery, there was another group of men digging a grave. There was not a woman in sight.

It was now the end of February, and we drove to a neighboring village named "Tatta" which was, according to our neighbor, "a tomato and onion sandwich and three Scotch and sodas away" from Karachi. Actually, it was 55 miles from Karachi and proved to be a veritable treasure house of Sind-style architecture. The fascinating old mosques and mausoleums were constructed of bricks upon which exquisite designs had been etched, glazed and kiln-baked before being used to construct the buildings. The experience of seeing the ancient buildings was eerie because it seemed as though there was nothing but graves, tombs and mausoleums for miles on the outskirts of the village. In one case, we were all allowed to enter a mosque. Judi, Joyce and I took our shoes off, which is what the men always do when they entered to pray. Judi and I felt very privileged. Women, because they menstruate, are considered to be unclean and are, therefore, seldom allowed in the mosques.

Sind was captured by the Arabs in 711 A.D. and remained in Muslim occupation until 1843 when it became a British possession. Architectural remains of that period were surprisingly few, primarily because the buildings were usually built of brick. Also, because the Indus River changed its course so often, no trace remains of the towns that were along its banks. During the period of 1627-1644, when Tatta was first included in the Mughal Empire, construction and carving in stone was attempted. The carvings, called "lacework in stone", were beautiful but because stone was difficult to procure, bricks and tiles came into use again.

We learned that of the 49 protected monuments in Sind, 17 are located in Tatta. We were sorry that we did not have time to visit them in depth as the monuments are said to be excellent examples of ancient Muslim architecture.

Even though we were short of time, we took a few minutes to tour the center of the village. We drove on a narrow, brick street, barely wide enough for our car to miss apartment house steps that bordered the edges. I shuddered to think what we would have done if a car had dared to come from the other direction!

The town is situated on a series of little hills, with houses built randomly throughout. They sprouted like relatively new mushrooms on an ancient landscape. I wanted to get out of the car and walk around to some of the bazaars, but Frank was anxious to leave. He turned off onto a side street, and headed back home, but not before clipping the side of the car slightly on somebody's door step.

A few days after we returned home, my neighbor sent over a chit (note) asking me to take her place on a Welfare Committee that was going to visit several charitable organizations to determine which one would be the most deserving recipient of monetary aid from the American Women's Club. We toured several places including a Health Center, staffed and manned by a club with a membership of 25 women. Under the direction of the Deputy Health Director, and through his training, these women, who were all in purdah (had veils over their faces) gave shots, administered to the sick in many ways, and furnished free milk to all of the children in their neighborhood. With their advice, we visited three special schools. We were astonished to see that the school for the blind was taught by a blind teacher; and the school for the deaf was taught by a deaf teacher. The deaf teacher said he could tell by the shape of his student's mouths and movement of their throats whether or not they were pronouncing their words correctly. Interestingly, most of these students, and the blind students, were taught at desks with attached seats, much like American desks, whereas, at most of the public Pakistani schools students sat cross-legged on the ground while they were being taught. The third special school that we visited was a home for delinquent boys. We were struck by the discipline, cleanliness and apparent good management of the three institutions.

Anxious to become involved, I joined several committees, a sketching class, and substituted at the American School on occasion.

Living in Karachi gave me an opportunity to experiment in activities that I had wanted to do but could not do earlier in my life. I had always been interested in painting. When some of my friends encouraged me to join a sketch club, I jumped at the chance, although with trepidation, because unlike my classmates, I had never had training in art. I began taking lessons from a man reputed to be one of Pakistan's best artists. If I hadn't known better, I would have sworn the man was Jesus. He had kind, loving features; long black hair hanging way below his shoulders, and a black beard and black mustache. He was dressed in a flowing robe of tan wool, white slacks and sandals. Did I ever wish I had been an accomplished artist. If ever there was a perfect subject, it was he!

One day the sketching model was a coolie woman, again a perfect subject. Coolies were the lowest caste, but were the most colorful. This one happened to be young and very pretty, wearing an array of color and patterns such as I had never seen. The top of her outfit, the sleeves and the part over her shoulder, was made of a red satin material with some sort of a pattern on it. Fastened to this were two "pockets" of purple and white fabric into which her breasts were nestled. Attached to these "pockets" was a piece of straight material hanging down over her stomach, much like a loin cloth, of a lavender fabric with a paisley print. Her back and stomach were bare with the exception of this cloth. Underneath this garment she wore a pair of shalwar pants, the full baggy pants that were so common, made of a striped material that had a floral design in between the stripes of red and yellow. Over her head and covering her bare back was a scarf of another shade of red, and with yet another pattern! On her arms were ivory bracelets dangling from the wrists nearly to the elbows; while on her ankles were big silver bracelets (about three), and on every toe were wide silver rings that extended to the end of her toes. She also wore a heavy silver necklace and huge silver ear rings. We must have looked terribly plain to her.

Later, I volunteered to help serve milk in a refugee camp. What an experience that was! Twice a week I mixed up a load of powdered milk in our *washing machine* and transferred the milk into a huge vat that was delivered by the Embassy carryall to our house. Embassy drivers had already picked up milk from the homes of two other volunteers. When the milk had been transferred, I piled into the carryall with the vats and the volunteers, and we headed for the Drigh Road Refugee Camp which was located about two miles from our house. Refugees of all ages, from small children to elderly and crippled, were eagerly waiting in long lines with all sorts of containers, including beer cans and wash tubs. With the help of Embassy personnel, we trudged over ruts and camel dung, dodging "pye" (wild) dogs, and slowly made our way to a makeshift distribution center where we poured milk into their containers. They went happily on their way, only to return a few days later for a repeat performance. This volunteer effort by the American Government was considered to be a successful project in which we were helping the indigent people—sort of like a small scale Marshall Plan, I thought. It was successful, until one day the project came to an abrupt halt when someone discovered that the refugees were not drinking the milk, but were selling it. They said the milk gave them a stomach ache.

Those activities provided endless opportunities for photographic sessions. One day, however, we were disappointed to get four rolls of film back to discover a note saying the film had been exposed to extreme heat. Oh, my gosh! I hoped all of our film hadn't been ruined. We had taken some pictures that probably couldn't be replicated. One was of a native butcher shop, where the meat was hanging out in the open and some men were sitting cross-legged on a table grinding hamburger. We thought for sure they would mix some toes and flies in with the ground meat! We shot another picture of an old woman who was washing clothes as she smoked her hukka pipe. A grizzled old man tapped me on the shoulder and pointed to the woman.

"Nay", he admonished.

"Nay?" I queeried. "Teaka. Nay."

I had said, "No? O.K., no." He was satisfied. Little did he know I had already taken the photo. I hoped it would turn out!

We also were able to get a photo of a child's funeral. The child, wrapped in a stark white sheet, was carried in a little red basket. It was another example of life's pathetic tragedies.

We took as many pictures as we possibly could—movies and stills—with color and with black and white film. The thought that some of them might not turn out was more than disappointing.

We were able to take some movies of a woman at a loom in her hut. She was not chanting as so many of them did, but rather the rhythmic clicking of the loom as she wove the red and yellow thread into a striped pattern was music in itself. She sat beside a pit into which were two bits of crude machinery which resembled the treadle of an old-fashioned sewing machine. One foot worked the treadle that held the red yarn; the other foot worked the treadle that held the yellow. In her hand was another crude device with which she formed the pattern. She offered to let me try my hand at the loom, but I quickly declined. It looked way too complicated.

She invited us into her hut, and I noticed the floor was hard clay which had been swept clean. There was no furniture save a charpoi (a crude cot with rope stretched back and forth between pieces of wood instead of bed springs) on its side against the clay wall. Inside her kitchen was a fire pit and a few crude utensils. Hovering near the fire pit was a lovely girl about 12, holding a naked baby as she comforted her squalling little four-year-old brother who was crying and tugging at her skirts because he was terrified of us.

As we departed, we ducked under some straw that was suspended about three feet above ground, into another room that held some smaller spinning wheels, across the sewer ditch, and into the real world again.

What to do about our bearer was a constant worry. He simply was not working out. I heard that there was an opening in the Metropolis Hotel for a room bearer, so before Shafi knew what was happening, I took him over to apply. Unfortunately, the job had already been filled. His chin plunged down to his boot tops when he realized why he was there; he was afraid of losing not only his job, but his face. We then had a long talk. He wanted to stay with us, but we decided that we were paying a lot of money to get Frank's shoes polished. We were unable to find another position for our "slower-than-molasses" bearer, so after he had been with us six months we packed him up and sent him back to his village.

Next we hired Aziz, a cook/bearer who although he was temperamental, turned out to be worth his weight in gold. Aziz was tall for a Pakistani, about 5'9", and skin and bones. His hair was salt-and-pepper; a small, neat mustache sprouted beneath his chiseled nose; and his cheek bones were clearly defined on his gaunt face. He had a serious, no-nonsense demeanor. I liked him immediately, and more importantly, so did Joyce. A lot!

Aziz turned out to be an excellent cook with only a few exceptions. His standards of cleanliness matched our own. Because he had always worked for British families, he had quite a bit to learn about American cookery but was a quick study. The only disappointing meal that he prepared for us happened shortly after his arrival. He had prepared lobster with mayonnaise one day and had a lot left over. So, as we were flying out the door to watch the American men's basketball team lose to the Punjabi team, I told him to cook up some macaroni and we would have macaroni salad with sliced tomatoes for dinner. The weather was hot—112 degrees—and a nice cold salad sounded so good that we invited a family of five to join us. We returned home to discover that the whole gooey mess had been cooking on the stove for three solid hours! It was my fault; I had neglected to tell him that we would have it cold. We ended up with tomato sandwiches for dinner along with mincemeat pie that had been swimming in too rich a crust. Aziz learned quickly, however, as evidenced by a dinner party we hosted a few nights later for 20 people without a hitch.

He didn't mind my puttering in the kitchen, so we worked together on many dishes. I taught him how to bake delicious bread, rolls and pastries, which saved me a considerable amount of work and time. The two kitchens were spic and span under his control. It was the hamal's job to do general work such as washing appliances, dusting and cleaning; the sweeper's job to clean the floors. Yet, Aziz got down on his hands and knees and did those chores himself in the kitchen, even going so far as to ask my husband to buy some whitewash so that he could whitewash the walls that had been blackened by the kerosene and coal stoves.

Two subjects that were always paramount in conversations amongst foreigners were 1) Karachi tummy and 2) black towels. I relented one day and gave Aziz some of our snowy white terry cloth towels to use for his hands in the kitchen. Several days later he was dusting with one of them. In a nice way, I suggested that he use them just for his hands because they wouldn't wear out so fast (trying to steer clear of the real reason) but he was very firm in telling me he would use the towel just that one time to dust with since it was dirty, and then he would have the dhobi wash it. The roof went off the next day, however, when at the same time, Aziz and I saw Abdullah drying dishes with the dirty towel. In unison, we chorused "NO" at the top of our lungs!

Although we had hired Shafi and Abdullah together, we kept Abdullah on against our better judgment when we let Shafi go. Poor Abdullah—even though he was a sweet old man and pleasant, we finally let him go, too. Not only were his standards not up to ours, but he reeked. His body odor was so bad that it permeated every room he worked in until long after he left it. We could stand it no more.

We didn't know exactly where Aziz, our cook/bearer lived, but he said it took him about 10 minutes to bicycle to work. One day he asked Frank if he could have a large wooden shipping crate that we had discarded. He explained that he wanted to use the wood to build a roof over his hut. He said he had lived in his hut for seven months and it had never had a roof over it. We couldn't imagine how he and his family could have existed without a roof over their heads, especially during the last few months with all of the rain Karachi had been having. The man across the street said since January 1954, in less than a month-long period, rainfall had already exceeded the usual annual amount! The poor refugees had already been rained out of their huts three times during the last month and still had the monsoon rains to contend with.

The third rain occurred on February 18, 1954, and included thunder and lightening that time. The rainfall we'd had three times the past month was said to be the first such rainfall (outside of the monsoon) in the entire history of this part of the country. The ground was a solid mass of murky lakes floating above clay-like soil. Water eventually evaporated out of the lakes rather than drained out. Neither this city, nor the people, were prepared for such rainfall. None of the streets had drains, and everything was a smelly mess. One day I noticed one of the main streets downtown was waist deep with water. One boy was taking a bath in it; another was washing his bicycle; a man was trying to pull his donkey and cart through it; while elsewhere, several children were having the time of their lives splashing around in it.

The people who shared the third portion of our house, spoke about being rescued by raft with their eight-day-old baby and four-year-old daughter when their former house was flooded during one of the monsoon rains the previous July. Needless to say, she and the four-year-old were terrified, and this experience may well have contributed to the nervous breakdown she had recently suffered.

Most of the refugees were squatters who settled on any available land they could find after they fled from India. Aziz told me there were 40 families (his family included) who had been squatting on some Pakistani army land since Partition, and now they had been given two day's notice to tear down their huts and move somewhere else. He had just finished building a roof over it with lumber that we gave him from our packing crate. To lose that, as well as any money he had put into his hut, would be tragic because in his limited circumstances an anna (2 cents) meant a lot more to him than a dollar did to us.

Two colonels had examined the property previously. "Let them stay," they said. "They aren't doing any harm."

Then along came the third colonel. "Get them out of here. This is not their property! I want them out of here," he screamed, slamming his fist on the table. "They have to be gone; every one of them. They have two days to get out of here!"

Aziz and his family were devastated (as were the others), so he came to me with tears in his eyes.

"Please, Madam, can you help us?" Aziz pleaded. "Seven months we have lived here. Seven months we give no one a bad time. Can you help, Madam? Please?"

We had recently joined an officer's club, so I asked a major, who was the manager, if there was someone he knew who could help the refugees. The major arranged for us to meet with the colonel in charge, but before doing so, Aziz took me over to see his hut and meet his family. His hut was sparse, but I was amazed at how nice and clean their place was. Although the floor was hard clay, it was swept clean; although the furnishings were sparse, they were tidy. Aziz and his wife had a big vegetable garden on the hillside and their cow and calf were contentedly grazing nearby. Aziz's begum and four of their five children met me at the front door. His wife, although very plain, was shy and pleasant. Their children, also very shy, were peeking out from behind their mother's skirt. I was surprised to see how nicely they were dressed; how polite they were.

"Salaam," I said.

"Salaam Alaykum," they giggled. Since they didn't know English, and I didn't know Urdu, that was the extent of our conversation. Except, we did have smiles. All of us!

After visiting briefly, we took our leave of Aziz's family and with apprehension, arrived within a few minutes at the colonel's military quarters where his begum greeted us. Aziz remained outside, squatting on the ground, while she ushered me into her pleasant surroundings. She was quite sympathetic and said she had pleaded with her husband to allow the refugees to stay.

"I have begged my husband to let them stay, but he won't listen to me. Will you please stay and talk to him?" she implored. "He will be home shortly. If you ask him to let them stay it will carry more weight than if I do," she said.

I ended up staying at the begum's house through a neighbor's visit; through a thorough education from two moral rearmament workers; practically lost my life, if not my patience, as a result of being constantly pinched, bumped and hit by the begum's son, whom she described as "retarded"; and finally, through a visit by a Pakistani couple who seemed familiar to me. It turned out that he was Habib, the Wing Commander of the Pakistani Air Force, whom we had met at a party in December, and who was a cousin of the man who built our Crazy House. Habib's sister, who had also been at the party, was a charming artist that I had frequently wished I could see again! The pleasant atmosphere that transpired wafted across the room like a soft feather as the colonel's begum realized that I had met her friends socially.

The colonel finally returned home about noon. He was very cordial because I was an American, which counted a lot in Pakistan in those days, and because Habib and I were having such a friendly conversation it took several minutes before I could state my business. Not that it mattered one iota. The colonel was unrelenting. Pleading with him served no purpose—none whatsoever! Aziz and the other refugees were kicked out of their huts and forced to find other quarters. In Aziz's case, it meant that his eldest son would stay with him, but his wife, four of their children, their cow and their calf would all have to go back to their village.

CHAPTER EIGHT

MAIL, DEPRESSION, ACTIVITIES

After that episode, Aziz was horribly depressed; almost as depressed as I had been ever since we arrived in Karachi. Mail was our only saving grace. I was so hungry for mail from home that even an advertisement looked good, providing it arrived with a good ole' American three-cent stamp on it.

My neighbor explained the process: "APO mail at regular postage takes six days to arrive from the day it is mailed in the States, but comes in only on Mondays, unless the pilots dump it somewhere like they did three weeks ago in order to carry a planeload of monkeys. Then we wait another week hoping it gets through the next time. International mail at 25 cents comes in on Tuesdays, Thursdays, and Saturdays," he continued, "but oftentimes isn't distributed until the next day, but at least it usually is delivered to the Embassy on time."

My friend, Berdina, responded more promptly than the Sears Catalog did by far. She would keep me informed about news from home, and would send me many things that I desperately needed (or thought I did.) I would send her a blank check and she would order important things that I wanted (like chewing gum or records) and have the stores ship the items. My sister, Carol, and other friends would also oblige. They were all wonderful; I was so appreciative to have this connection with home.

Our household goods finally arrived on December fifth, and our car on January sixth. We felt as though we had been liberated until we got some heartbreaking news. We received word that Frank's brother, Ernie, had died of esophageal cancer on February 18. He was Frank's only sibling, and the news was a real shock to us.

Frank flew to Pennsylvania immediately to attend Ernie's funeral and comfort his widow, his brother's three sons and his parents, who had traveled East from Spokane. The children and I stayed behind, shivering in the icy-cold Karachi winter. During the time that Frank was away the temperatures were between 59 and 70 degrees during the day. But our house, which was built entirely of cement with no interior heat, saw to it that we were miserably uncomfortable during the nights because our blood was so thin.

April had now arrived and the parties continued unabated; there had been no let up since the holidays. One night we were mentioned as "two of Karachi's elite" by the *Dawn* newspaper, who were guests at the birthday celebration given by the Ambassador of Japan and Mrs. Tagamoto in honor of His Majesty, the Emperor of Japan. Next to the Nixon's reception, it was the biggest and most colorful event we had attended. Among the 500 guests were Cabinet Ministers, Chiefs of Diplomatic Missions, civil and military officials, members of the diplomatic corps, the Mayor of Karachi, and crème` de la crème` of Karachi society. Lovely artificial flowers adorned the surroundings; Japanese lanterns swayed in the breeze while a band played Japanese tunes. Not infrequently, we noticed Americans staring at the Japanese flag; a flag that was still difficult for us to accept after the Pearl Harbor disaster.

We couldn't help but be impressed by elaborate parties such as the Japanese reception, but one of the most enjoyable social events that we had the pleasure of attending was a good old American barbecue that was held on the roof of a house across the street from ours. Using a portable grill, they barbecued beef patties, and served hamburgers with all of the trimmings. Delicious! The servants thought we had lost our minds. Who on earth had ever heard of cooking on a roof before? However, the roofs were perfect for entertaining when it was hot. Roofs were cooler than indoors, and most of them were large and flat; not ours of course. Since it was the Crazy House, even the roof had its different levels. If we had dared to cook on our roof, we would have had to play leap frog while doing so.

The day before school opened we took the children for their first swim in the Arabian Sea. What a treat! The salty ocean water was lukewarm and a joy to play in. Swimming was forbidden from June until late September because of the dangerous waters caused by strong monsoon winds, and because of annual onslaughts of poisonous blue fish that paralyze people they touch, sometimes fatally. Not even our house could escape the ravages of the wind. Although the winds caused a lot of sand to blow into our house, they helped cool down the sweltering heat in the process.

We also took our first camel ride on the beach. What an experience! The front end went one way, while the back end went the other as the camel, chewing its cud, loped easily with squashy hooves on the hot sand. The experience was not unlike that of riding in a rocking chair; a *high* rocking chair.

We began to take weekly trips to the beach. Imagine a *lukewarm* Pacific Ocean! The Arabian Sea, a part of the Indian Ocean, was safe to swim and play in most of the year. When I swam in the Arabian Sea there were occasions when I wondered if I could get up again or not. One time, a wave knocked me under and dragged me on the sand, giving me a badly skinned knee; the next time, two big waves collided, rolling me around underwater a couple of times to the left, then a couple of times to the right, before slamming me down on the sand. It was frightening; frightening because I had no control. Some witnesses said the trouble was caused by two big waves that came together in back of me.

The Embassy personnel built a tennis court a block from our house, so Frank and I began playing tennis once in awhile. We wanted to play while the weather was dry because the court was paved with camel dung; imagine what it would be like after a rain! We also tried to play when the weather was cool. One day we began playing at 7:00 a.m., and were dripping wet when we finished at 8:00 a.m. Every stitch of our clothing was soaked.

Judi and Doug had adjusted nicely, especially Doug. He fit right in wherever he went, and always found a lot of things to keep him occupied. Judi found quite a different life for herself than she had in the States. So many of her friends were either older than she was, or else because of years of "foreign life" were older than their years. When they had get-togethers, it was always for dinner and usually included ballroom dancing. She had learned to jitterbug and when the USS Pittsburgh was in port she had her first dance with a sailor. After being intimidated for a few seconds she danced beautifully, and I was pleased for her sake.

Later, she planned her 13th birthday party jointly with a friend, but at the friend's house. We gave her a gorgeous Gruen watch that a Denver friend selected for her. She had wanted a watch for ever so long, and we knew she would be happy with this one. She had done very little baton twirling. She gave a few performances for various groups, but it was simply too hot to practice. However, she was thrilled to receive a copy of the national *Drum Major Magazine* to discover her picture on the cover, and a story inside about her move to Pakistan.

Judi was popular among her peers. She spent a lot of time riding her bicycle, learning to jitterbug and ballroom dance, and participating in school activities. She had never caused a discipline problem, so it was quite a shock to me when she intentionally locked one of her teachers in the KAS bathroom. Neither Judi nor I remember why she locked her in (except that she could), how long the teacher was locked in, or what the consequences were. I am sure she was punished. I know I was mortified.

Doug was likeable, gregarious, and hyperactive. He knew everything and everybody worth knowing for miles around, and I mean miles because, consumed with curiosity, he rode his bicycle all over Karachi, even hitching rides onto the back ends of camel and donkey carts just as the natives did while riding his bike. He also developed a habit of exploring caves. On one occasion he picked up a sick bat which promptly bit him on his ear and on his thumb. Of course, Doug didn't tell us what had happened and I didn't learn about that activity until long after we returned to the States. What if he had contracted rabies? What if there had been a nest of kraits (snakes) waiting to bite him? The "what ifs" were endless. I would have died a thousand deaths had I known what he was doing.

CHAPTER NINE

TOP NOTCH CALVERT EDUCATION

A major concern that we had regarding our assignment in Pakistan was the possibility of inadequate or inferior education for the children. These concerns proved to be groundless, however. Judi and Doug enrolled in the Karachi-American Society School, a school that was specifically designed for the benefit of children living abroad.

On January 20, 1953, the community school, which was located 1½ blocks from our house, had been established with an enrollment of 33 children and a staff of five teachers. Judi and Doug enrolled 11 months later on November 2 that first year. There were eight students in Judi's class and three in Doug's when they started. By spring of the following year, the enrollment stood at 92 children spread between eight grades plus kindergarten, with plans to add 9th and 10th grade classes in September, and possibly an 11th grade class if demand warranted it.

In 1954, there were approximately 50 students enrolled in the Karachi American Society School, but Doug's class of four had dwindled to one and that student was Doug. By April, 1955, 55 families were represented at the school—11 students were connected to the American Embassy, 14 to FOA (our group), nine to the U.S. Armed Forces, eight to the Ford Foundation, 10 to private businesses, and three to miscellaneous organizations.

In less than three years, the original enrollment of 33 students increased to 200 students, with further expansion coming in the near future. The education they were receiving was excellent, and in Doug's case amounted to private tutoring. (After we returned to the States, we discovered that they were ahead by one year of stateside students in their subjects.) The school cost us 65 rupees a month for each child, or about $45 a month for both of them. Students missed some subjects, such as music and art, although from time to time volunteers filled the void and they were able to make up the difference.

Students were taught by the Calvert System, an accredited correspondence system headquartered in Baltimore, Maryland, and which operated in Karachi with a professional staff that was assisted by volunteers.

The staff included the principal, a business manager, 10 full-time teachers (some of whom were parents, some not, but most with professional training), three part-time teachers for singing, music theory and painting, and numerous volunteers for activities such as sports, square dancing and scouts. Servants included a bearer (with duties equivalent to a school janitor) who was on duty whenever there were children in the building, a combination gardener and night watchman, and a sweeper who assisted the bearer.

Doug and Judi were both straight A students, and enjoyed the intimacy of the small American School. They went to school from 7:30 a.m. to noon, so were finished before the hottest time of the day. When the heat increased in April, the school day ended at 11:30 a.m. On May 28, it closed for the summer, not to reopen until the first week of October.

KAS was governed by the Karachi American Society. Its aim, as clearly stated in their Articles of Association, was not to create an American "island" in Pakistan, nor to insulate their children from fruitful association with children of other nationalities, but to create a cultural and educational center in order "to promote a spirit of good fellowship and international understanding through informal instruction, recreational and cultural activities" open to children and adults alike.

A lot of square dancing for both groups took place, and a variety of other activities, including fundraisers, were held. One delightful fundraiser was a Sadie Hawkins dinner dance. The "invites" for that event went something like this:

"Kin U cum 2 R Sadie Hawkins Sosechul dance. Thar will be vitals (scuse pleze, no poke chops), we uns will fernish the corn; U all bring yer own likker."

The evening was hilarious.

The school moved its location a couple of times in the first few months owing to various factors such as an expanding enrollment and falling ceilings. It originally was housed in the home of Principal and Mrs. Al Wilson of the Ford Foundation. When living accommodations for the Wilson family of five were reduced to one bedroom, it was determined that the school and the Wilsons deserved separate buildings. By late November 1954, the new location was overgrown, and the school was then moved again, this time into a two-story mansion that had originally been designed to house two families. It provided the school with 10 classrooms, seven bathrooms, principal's office, kitchen, storerooms, verandahs, patio, a compound for sports, two garages for scout meetings and a roof for square dancing.

One day my neighbor asked if I would take her place on a committee from the American Women's Association that was investigating organizations in order to determine which one would be the most deserving to receive a monetary gift from them.

We visited a number of institutions in the neighborhood, and then evaluated three special schools. We were astonished to discover that the school for the blind was taught by a blind teacher; and the school for the deaf was taught by a deaf teacher! The deaf teacher said he could tell by the shape of his student's mouths and movement of their throats whether or not they were pronouncing their words correctly. Interestingly, most of these students, as well as the blind students, were taught sitting at desks that had attached seats, similar to American desks, whereas, at most of the public Pakistani schools students were taught as they sat cross-legged on the ground. The third special school that we visited was a home for delinquent boys. We were struck by the discipline, cleanliness and apparent good management of the three institutions.

At first I declined an offer to teach school (on a volunteer basis) because I preferred staying home with Joyce; but later I agreed to teach the kindergarten class when I learned she could come with me. I hated to be involved in anything that kept me away from her every morning. This new arrangement was the perfect solution; we could both go to kindergarten!

Anxious to become involved, I joined several committees, a sketching class, and substituted at the American School when they needed help. I did a fine job with the kindergarten group, but failed miserably when it came to substituting as a math teacher!

The trouble started when I was asked to substitute for the 5th grade math class.

"I don't mind teaching, I just don't think I know 5th grade math," I admitted. They thought I was kidding. I wasn't.

The school officials assured me there would be no problem. "The kids have had it all before. It's simply review."

"Well, in that case . . ."

The math hour arrived and to my horror the students didn't know how to change decimals to fractions, or fractions to decimals. The brightest child in the class was Susan Bell, daughter of Mary and David Bell (we square danced with the Bells—Dave was head of the Ford Planning Commission, and later served as Budget Director of the United States during the Kennedy administration).

"I know how to do the hard ones, but how do you do the easy ones?" Susan asked. I bolted out the door and found a teacher who could help them.

"I hate going to school over here," Susan said.

"But, honey, you'd study the same subjects in the States," I said, trying to console her.

"Yes, but in the States the teacher would know!"

I felt so sorry for her. She was absolutely right! Luckily, her regular teacher soon returned from home leave and Susan was able to get the help that she needed.

Then there was Doug's experience when he was in the fifth grade. We were astounded to learn after reading his report card that he hadn't been doing his homework. That had never happened before. I met with his teacher (who was substituting while his regular teacher was on home leave) and she spent the entire time telling me how horrible he was, he didn't do anything right, and ended by saying, "I've tried everything with that child but nothing works."

"Have you tried liking him?" I asked, quietly.

"Well, er, ah, yes, ahem, that is—" and her voice trailed off into nothing—as empty as her understanding.

We met at a cocktail party a few days later and she said everything was fine. The next time I saw her, she said things couldn't have been worse. "Why yesterday he brought his paper and slammed it on the desk in front of me," she complained.

It had taken Doug to the third grade—and the kindly guidance of a wonderful teacher—before Doug recovered from the damage that a personality clash with a first-grade teacher had done to him. I was determined that no teacher could do that to him again.

One thing led to another as our voices grew louder.

"Are you insinuating that I am not a good teacher?" she demanded.

"I didn't say that, but I am saying that I think you lack understanding. I think the problem is a personality one," I said, my voice rising. "Doug suffered enough from his first grade experience, and I will take him back to the States before I will allow that to happen again."

"I won't have you sending him back on my account!" she screamed.

"You'll have nothing to say about it!" I screamed back, louder and angrier than I had ever been in my life.

We ended our exchange by agreeing to meet with the principal of the school, who deserved a medal for the way he handled two irate females.

Instead of the terrible, awful, uncooperative brat who couldn't and wouldn't do anything right, he was now "this dear, sweet boy I am trying so desperately to help."

The school's principal, Al Wilson, came to the house ostensibly to visit but for the purpose of evaluating Doug. He determined there was no problem. "Doug is a bright, charismatic young man," Al said. "The problem is not the child." The upshot was that Doug would stay in her class, but could essentially ignore the teacher, and the teacher agreed to do the same insofar as Doug was concerned.

At one point, the teacher told Frank, "Well, apparently you all think *I* am the problem!"

"Now you're getting the point," Frank retorted. Ten days later Doug's regular teacher returned from home leave. End of problem. We learned some time later that the substitute teacher had applied for a full-time teaching position but it was denied because her inadequacies were well known by authorities.

Shortly afterwards I was selected to be on a committee to choose a new school board, an enjoyable and not too time-consuming assignment. At this point, I was not only the proud natural mother of my three children, but the "adopted mother" of a puppy, two baby bunnies, three parrots, and 11 kindergartners.

Having the pets was a godsend. Doug had captured a wild, crippled parrot, so I thought if I bought him a pair of birds he would release the first one. Instead, we had three. The same day, some friends who were leaving for the states, came in with the cutest pair of bunnies; one was black and white; the other was tan and white. Frank didn't speak to me for quite a while after that 'adoption'. He wouldn't say no when I asked him if he cared if the children had them, but pouted for some time after they joined our family.

The first year or so that we were in Karachi was probably harder on Doug than on the rest of us. He had so few playmates. As June 2, 1954 approached, he celebrated his 10th birthday by inviting his friends on a turtle hunt. It was great fun to build bonfires on bright, moonlit nights and barbecue hamburgers and hot dogs while we waited for the female turtles to waddle up on the beaches during a full moon to lay their eggs. The turtles weighed between 200 and 300 pounds. They were huge; so huge that Doug and some of the other kids could ride them.

On one occasion we brought one of the turtles home, named her Suzie, and laid her on her back so that she couldn't crawl away. What to do with her now that we had her home? There was no way we were going to kill her and make turtle soup, nor were we going to give her to a hotel so that their chef could make a gourmet delicacy out of her meat. We kept her on her back for two days, but couldn't stand to look into her sad eyes. We finally piled her into the Jeep and drove her back to the ocean and released her. None of us will ever forget how, as soon as she was out of the Jeep, she raised her head, sniffed, and made a bee-line for the ocean. I can't begin to tell you how good—how relieved—we all felt that we had set her free. We watched her with tears in our eyes until she ducked out of sight beneath a big wave.

Silently, we began driving home along the desert road that was abloom with spring flowers. The flowers in Karachi were gorgeous. The bougainvillea were luxuriant; the marigolds, phlox, sweet williams, sweet peas, poppies, and hollyhocks were as colorful as rainbows as they reached full bloom in March; and the banyan trees were covered with sensational red blossoms. The poinsettias were spectacular; as large as dinner plates and more beautiful than most of the plates that graced our tables.

It was one thing to admire the beautiful blossoms; another thing to walk in the fields between the houses where clay crumbled under our feet and we could trip over gopher holes. We had to carefully avoid clumps of sage brush because hidden in their shade were kraits, snakes about 10 to 12 inches long with venom so deadly that people were said to have died within 30 seconds after being bitten.

The sight of lepers and beggars was commonplace and provided a strong contrast to the lovely flowers. One day we visited a leper colony and were filled with compassion but also repulsion at the sights that we witnessed. Arms and legs and parts of bodies or faces were missing on some of the victims; others were fitted with wagon-like contraptions fastened to their bodies so that they could wheel themselves around. We would often see these people begging on the sidewalks in Karachi. We were filled with pity for them, but filled with apprehension, too, because we weren't sure how contagious leprosy was.

Occasionally we would see police dragging prisoners through town for violations such as non-payment of debt, stealing, or murder. One day they took our chowkidar away in chains. We never did know why.

I was never afraid of the Pakistani men, except once. One day I was squeezed between hordes of people in Bori Bazaar when something hard poked me in the back. I thought it was a stick. I turned around to glare at the man behind me—the one in the clean, light blue shalwar pants and kamiz (overblouse) who was pressing with all of his might on my back. As soon as I shot him a dirty look, he spun quickly around and disappeared into the crowd. His actions were not honorable, nor were his intentions!

CHAPTER TEN

INTERNATIONAL RECREATION PROGRAM

One day, Doug complained, "Mom, I've read three books in two days." It occurred to some of us that families in our community needed meaningful activities to keep them busy. Clearly something had to be done so when the president of the Karachi American Society School Board asked me if I would consider organizing and directing an international recreation program in cooperation with KAS, I jumped at the chance. I had worked as a volunteer with a similar program when I was president of the Young Married Women's Club of the Denver YWCA a few years earlier and gained experience which proved to be invaluable for this venture.

I started by sending questionnaires to all members of the American Community asking them to indicate their areas of interest. From the results, the Recreational Program was born. It included as many as 18 activities each week with a total participation of approximately 550 persons. In addition to Americans, Pakistanis, and Parsees, there were participants from nine other countries.

At one point, the schedule included four bridge classes, three ballroom dancing classes, and four Indian dancing classes. Other weekly classes included painting, Indian drums, creative writing, swimming, horseback riding, cooking, photography, tap dancing, carpentry, archery, baton twirling, cartooning, and more. Judi taught baton twirling, Frank taught carpentry, and I taught cartooning. What a laugh! I had never drawn a cartoon in my life, but I had a wonderful book. I practiced before each lesson and the students (and I) loved the classes.

The program was entirely self-supporting. Judi, Frank and I, and some of the other instructors, volunteered our time; some of the other instructors were paid a small salary. I was paid a small salary for directing the program, which helped pay the cost of our servants. The program was successful beyond our wildest dreams, albeit not without the usual frustrations of living in Karachi. For example, because of a shortage of telephones, I had to make countless personal calls all over the city. I had difficulty finding qualified instructors, and we needed to do a lot of borrowing because there was a shortage of equipment such as record players, records, and bridge tables. However, the enthusiasm of the participants cured any headaches that I may have encountered in the process.

Along with that activity, our friends, the Governor General's Aides de Camp, offered to let Josie Armstrong and me ride their horses three mornings a week. What an exhilarating experience it was for me to ride Shiny's dapple grey on the sand dunes that bordered the Arabian Sea. The warm tropical breezes blew my hair and kissed my cheeks, and I felt as though I were in heaven. So much so that when Shiny (the Aide de Camp in charge of the stables) offered to sell the dapple grey to me for only $300, I seriously considered it. I knew nothing about taking care of horses, and that realization was the only thing that prevented me from buying it. I learned later that he was trying to sell the horse because it was going lame in one leg!

There was a lot of interest in horseback riding in Karachi. The elite Pakistanis are accomplished equestrians and horseback riding was a popular class on the Recreation Program's curriculum. So, after several people asked if I would consider establishing our own KAS Riding Academy, fate intervened. I was in the process of determining whether such a project were feasible, when Frank came home and announced that we would be returning to the States within a few weeks. Luckily, the KAS Riding Academy had not progressed beyond the research stage. Can't you see what a mess we would have been in if we had had a stable full of horses to contend with as we were leaving town?

The KAS Recreational Program attracted the attention of Jaya Bolt, staff writer for the Dawn Newspaper, who wrote a long feature story. She said in part:

> *It is customary to hear complaints about Karachi and its enervating climate—how it is a trial to women, how they become languid, inert and debilitated. Not so American women. Judging*

from their numerous activities in the City, it seems to make them unusually strenuous and enterprising.

One of them, Mrs. Frank Tessitor for instance, has in the space of six months organized a recreational program for the Karachi-American Society with classes in almost any hobby one may have a fancy for—unless it is something as extravagant as underwater photography. Mrs. Tessitor offers an impressive list of eighteen different activities, open to all nationalities and including classes in Square Dancing, Painting, Cooking, Photography, Horseback Riding, Bridge and even Archery. There are already 275 participants of about nine nationalities.

The feature story was lovely, but nicer yet was a letter I received from Sally Pfeiffer, President of the Board of Directors of the Karachi-American Society, in response to my letter of resignation when we announced that we were returning home:

Were it not that you are soon to leave Karachi no Board of Directors in its right collective mind would ever accept your letter of resignation. It is hard, if not impossible, to picture anyone else capable of having done the job you have done this year. The imagination and inventiveness with which you have developed the various facets of the Recreation Program combined with the long tedious hours you have spent tracking down instructors and delinquent bill-payers together add up to a unique achievement. To find creativeness plus a meticulous attention to detail in the same person is as rare as it is desirable and the success of the Recreation Program is in large part attributable to this combination of characteristics in the person of its director.

I know I can speak for the other members of the Board in saying that it has been a great pleasure for all of us to work with you this year, and to thank you not only for the job you have done in setting up the Recreation Program, but also for giving us the benefit of your advice at innumerable Board meetings.

Sincerely, Sally Pfeiffer, President
Karachi-American Society Board of Directors

Our involvement with people of so many nationalities, and the activities which we offered in the KAS Recreation Program, were certainly highlights of our stay in Karachi. The longer we remained in this foreign post the more we enjoyed it (despite its drawbacks; one of which was constant concern for our health.)

In addition to our friendship with so many foreign friends, we had enjoyed going to the beach nearly every Sunday, oftentimes with them, to swim in the Arabian Sea. We would certainly miss our friends, and we would miss the lukewarm Indian Ocean.

CHAPTER ELEVEN

SICKNESS, BUGS, AND FRUSTRATIONS

During our Karachi tour, we were constantly aware that there was a lot of sickness in the city. In 1954, several of our friends either had contracted or were recovering from malaria or typhoid fever. Aziz, our cook/bearer, had just recovered from a serious bout of malaria; our sweeper's wife was not expected to live; we suspected that the sweeper had syphilis; our dhobi quit in the middle of the wash and lay half-dead on our garage floor. We were waiting for Frank to get home so that we could take the dhobi, his wife and five kids to the hospital because they all were suffering with malaria-type symptoms. There was a high incidence of malaria and yellow jaundice early in 1954, and small pox and typhoid fever had reached epidemic proportions in the refugee camps. Malaria had been rare in Karachi, but suddenly the disease was rampant.

Then at our house, there was the usual—Judi spent two days with a severe upset stomach; Doug had been suffering from a bad cold for several days, and Frank had been sick with a sunstroke after he had gone swimming in the ocean and played a strenuous game of handball on the beach afterwards.

Four Americans within a radius of one block in any direction of our house had fallen victims to yellow jaundice, which we were told is a symptom, not an illness. Two of the Americans had malaria along with the jaundice; the other two had hepatitis.

Frank thought I had either malaria or yellow jaundice because for three weeks I didn't feel well, was listless, and had little energy. After three days of tests my doctor determined that I had low blood pressure and an intestinal disorder called "Lamblia Giardia", which fortunately wasn't the amoebic variety.

Joyce had been developing periodic fevers which her doctor said were caused from tonsillitis. She was usually good at keeping herself occupied with crayons, paints, artwork, and playing with Ellen, the little girl next door, but when she was sick, her usual sunny disposition dropped to cranky and whiny and there was no living with her. When she felt better, having the bunnies to wheel around in her doll buggy with Mem Sahib, our dachshund pup, nipping at her heels gave her hours of pleasure and me some respite. It wasn't long before our dachshund (not yet a year old) was in heat and before we knew it, I was helping deliver five Springer Spaniel pups.

We prevailed upon one of our servants to stay with Joyce during one of her illnesses while we slipped away to attend a party next door. It was given by an American secretary who was taking care of our neighbor's portion of the Crazy House while they were on home leave. We ate a lovely dinner, enjoyed some dancing, and met the secretary's fiancée, a handsome Pakistani, Captain Sayeed Khan, who was the Governor General's Chief Bodyguard and who subsequently became a good friend of ours. He had unusually fine contacts, which included open-ended access to the G.G. beach hut and private yacht. I couldn't leave Joyce the way she felt, but Frank jumped at Sayeed's invitation to take Judi and Doug fishing on the G.G.'s yacht the following day.

Two days later, Frank stayed with Joyce while I took two couples for a pre-arranged swim at Melir, the Pakistani Officer's Club that we had joined, and which had been built by American servicemen and enjoyed by our friend from Denver who was teasing me about the big bugs in Karachi.

While we were swimming in the pool, some other Americans arrived, including two of the women in my sketching class. Before I knew it, an "artists' party" had been arranged for the next night at our house. One of the women was in charge of bringing invitations to three of the local artists. The invitations read "Can you leave your (and here I drew a picture of a palette) long enough to satisfy your palate?" One of the artists was Sheik Ahmed, my teacher; another was Ismaili, a portrait artist and engineer who worked with Frank and who later painted a magnificent portrait of Doug; and the third was Ahmed Parvez, an abstractionist, from whom I had purchased a lovely abstract painting. Surprisingly, the eight women in the pool were all available to attend our dinner on such short notice.

Could the artists attend? That was a little trickier, because there were so few telephones. Lucy brought invitations to two of the artists the next morning, but couldn't find where the third one lived. An hour before dinner Lucy and I went to Sheik Ahmed's house to see if he knew where Ishmaili lived, only to discover that Sheik had not yet seen his invitation. He changed his shirt in a hurry and took us to find Ishmaili's place. We got there 20 minutes before dinner, and by then we were laughing so hard we were almost in hysterics. I handed Ishmaili his invitation and said, "Read it quickly. You're invited to dinner in 20 minutes."

To our amazement, he could make it too! It turned out to be one of the most delightful parties we had ever given. Everyone agreed it should happen more often. It was such a gay affair that Frank, who didn't smoke, smoked not one but *two* cigarettes, announcing that he might as well "go all the way."

Contrary to the warnings of our Denver friend about the huge bugs in Karachi, we had seen very few, until one night when we hosted two tables of bridge. It was too hot to close the door (it had been 114 degrees during the day) and bugs swarmed under the screen door. By the time our guests left, the walls, lamps, floors, and furniture were solidly plastered with flying ants. We had had a terrible storm with thunder, lightening and rain pelting down in sheets that afternoon causing the siege of flying ants. According to the newspaper, it rained 1.13 inches within a few hours. Twelve people were killed and 35 injured when a wall collapsed in a refugee development, and the next day, the streets were flooded because of the nonporous, clay soil. I guess the flying ants needed some refuge.

We tried to eat hamburgers on the porch one night. Within two minutes and roughly 1,000 flies later, we flew into the house. Eating on the porch? Bad idea!

Frank, who had returned from a 10-day trip to Dacca, East Pakistan, a few nights earlier, said, "They have the biggest bugs I have ever seen! We had to turn our plates upside down until just before we put food on them, or else they would have been covered with huge bugs and flies. Then we had to gulp down the food really fast or the bugs would have eaten the food first."

On another occasion, Mrs. Hildreth, the American ambassador's gracious wife and Mamie Eisenhower look-alike, called a meeting to help

American wives learn how to take care of our foodstuffs in Karachi's tropical weather. I rushed home from the meeting and began tossing canned goods out of the storeroom (which had made a better incubator for eggs than a storeroom for canned pork and gravy). I then enlisted Frank's help in building shelves in the 'swimming pool' (the room that seeped water—still did). Now, our canned goods were down to a lower, cooler level, and I was grateful to have the shelves that Frank built, something the carpenter had promised for six months. Thus, our "swimming pool" now had built-in air conditioning. That was a good thing because it wasn't so dependent on our temperamental electrical system. For example, the power had been off from 9 a.m. to 5 p.m. the previous day; it was off again the next morning at 7 a.m. so there was no power, no water, no air conditioning—in short, no comfort!

It seemed as though every day brought forth a new experience. Judi had planned to go bunderboating with a large group, but through a mix-up they neglected to pick her up. To ease her feelings, we decided to try to find Manghopir, a town 11 miles outside of Karachi, which was famous not only for a shrine built on a high, rocky hill but for its hot water sulfur springs and tank which contained sacred crocodiles. Since we didn't know exactly where the town was, we traveled on many unfamiliar streets. There were so many interesting sights that it took us an hour and a half to get out of town—not that we got lost, but we stopped so many times to take pictures, and almost got mobbed everywhere we stopped by natives who wanted to have their pictures taken. We found the crocodiles, about 30 of them, in a moat-like area. Some were crawling on the ground; others were sleeping in the sun; and still others were swimming in the murky water with their huge jaws open, revealing ferocious-looking teeth as they snapped at bugs or fish. It was comforting to know that they were safely ensconced behind a big, rock wall, because we were told they were as vicious as they looked, and they looked vicious!

When we returned home I asked Aziz if he would please make some ice cream. He hit the ceiling! He completely lost his temper and stormed out of the house. It almost broke our hearts. We had liked him and his work so much, but we were at a loss to know what had upset him this time.

He returned two days later, apologized, and said he hadn't been able to think straight for the past month because he had so many worries. First, he had his hut taken away from him, then his wife and four children (who had gone back to their village) became very ill with typhoid fever. His 17-year-old son (who was living with him) became ill with malaria. The night I asked him to make ice cream he had hoped to finish work early to take his son to the doctor. I was unaware of his problems, so rather than tell us about them, he reached the end of his ropes and exploded. After he got his problems off of his chest he relaxed and said he didn't want to leave us.

I was aware that Aziz had been trying for several weeks to bring his wife and four of his five children back to Karachi from their village. One morning I asked him if she was going to be able to come to Karachi or not.

"No, Madam. She no come."

"Why not, Aziz?"

"Scuze me please, Madam, but three years ago I take other wife and–"

"You mean you have two wives?" I blurted out, incredulous. He had worked for us for the past 10 months and had never mentioned having a second wife. But that explained why he had dyed his hair black from salt and pepper in anticipation of his wife's arrival, and why he had built purdah quarters. He was preparing for the arrival of his second (and younger) wife! "Yes, Madam. Now second wife has moved in with first wife and first wife don't like it. Second wife say if first one come to Karachi, she will come too. First wife's brother write me and say if I take second one with me, first wife give kids to me but she no come with it. But second wife no want the kids."

"I also wrote a letter to second wife's father asking him to say he was taking his daughter to another village." Aziz continued. "From there, I will see that she makes it to Karachi."

"What does Latif [Aziz's son] say about that?" I asked.

"I don't ask. He no like it," Aziz said.

"But what if he writes and tells his mother that Wife #2 is with you?" I persisted.

"I take chance, Madam," he said, shrugging his shoulders in a sign of resignation.

"That's a shame, Aziz," I said, still in a state of shock. "Do you have children by wife Number 2?"

"Only one girl. Another baby die when she three month s old."

"I'm sorry, Aziz." I said.

Love in the Muslim world was almost unknown as we know it. Most marriages are arranged by the parents, as was Aziz's first marriage when he was 17 years old. He said his second wife was 19 when they married. I was overcome with curiosity, and asked him if he married her because he was in love with her. He didn't understand my question. "I mean, do you like her."

"Yes, I like it."

"Which wife do you like better?"

"I like it both, Madam. My first wife never spend money; always sew and make things for the girls. Second wife want good time too much. Always want to go to picture show and like that. My first wife don't like it."

I was stunned at this revelation. Although Muslims are permitted four wives, I couldn't believe this man, who already had a lot of problems, would take on another wife; take on more problems! I had often wondered how married women felt when their husbands took on additional wives, and was amused to notice that jealousy wasn't limited to our race alone. I also asked him if his wives were in purdah [veils over their faces].

"Yes, Madam."

"Why, Aziz? Why are your wives in purdah?"

"Because I say so!" he snapped.

Again I was shocked. Our cook/bearer apparently thought nothing of taking orders from me, an American woman (or was he just good at hiding his contempt?) Certainly, when it came to his own women, his thinking and customs were those of ancient beliefs. I was totally surprised that he could be so dictatorial when it came to them.

Pakistan was slowly adopting some western customs. Coca Cola was one of the American businesses which began to take an interest in the new country. They opened a bottling plant in Karachi, which was sparkling clean with sterilized bottles. But, teaching sanitary procedures to the wallas who served the cokes was as difficult as teaching camels to stop at red lights. One day, after a trip to the library, Judi's teacher treated her students to a coke. The walla (vendor) opened the coke bottle and poured the liquid into a dirty glass. Judi's teacher and the students were appalled!

"No! No! No!" their teacher shouted, gesticulating wildly.

The walla said, "Teaka, Mem Sahib. Teaka." (O.K., Mrs., O.K.)

He then grabbed a dirty, rusty funnel and calmly proceeded to pour the Coca Cola back into the bottle! The horrified teacher grabbed a bottle opener and opened 10 bottles herself so the students could drink straight from the bottles. We later learned that some of the wallas filled used bottles with other liquids and sold them as Coca Cola. Then there was the time that two of our guests complained that their cocktails tasted of kerosene. Apparently one of the soft drink bottles had contained more than soft drinks at some point.

Once again our mail delivery system was the bearer of bad news. My sister, Carol Pollock, wrote that her second child, six-year-old Kim, had contracted polio. He had been hospitalized for six weeks, and had been paralyzed from the waist down. She said his attitude was good, and since her last letter telling us about his illness (which we didn't receive) he could now move one leg a little bit, and had been able to stand for one second with them holding him. With extensive therapy Kim progressed until he could walk with crutches.

It was hard to be so far away. I began to consider moving to California when we returned to the States in case I could be of some help to my sister.

CHAPTER TWELVE

HURRY UP AND WAIT

"Mr. Tessitor, the Pakistan Government is asking if we could send them someone with your qualifications to help them set up and equip a soil mechanics and hydraulics research laboratory in Karachi," the State Department voice had said. "If you are willing to accept this assignment, it will be for two years, but you will have to leave immediately." The challenge Frank accepted turned out to be a five-year tour for him, not two, and because the request was so urgent, he departed for Pakistan as soon as he finished his indoctrination.

It was now April 1954, and we had been in Karachi seven months. It had been nine months since Frank had received the *urgent* request from the Department of State in Washington, D.C., to proceed to Pakistan at *your earliest.* While he was waiting for Pakistani red tape to unravel, he had completed all of the arrangements for the designing and ordering of equipment for the new laboratory and had been working on a variety of other projects at the behest of his superior. To his consternation, he had been unable to establish the hydraulics research laboratory to which he had been assigned because the Pakistani government was still trying to decide if they wanted to fund it! Once they reached a decision, it took considerable time for them to find property upon which to erect the building.

Frank, a mechanical engineer who had been working at civil and hydraulic engineering for the U.S. government, was dedicated to his work. He had worked on Bonneville, Grand Coulee and Boulder (Hoover) Dams for the U.S. Bureau of Reclamation prior to launching a 12-year stint as a hydraulic engineer and materials investigator in charge of the Bureau of Reclamation Testing Materials Laboratory in Denver, Colorado.

After leaving Denver in the middle of July 1953, he flew to Washington, D.C. Pakistan was so anxious to have him over there immediately, that someone in Washington thought he should skip indoctrination and proceed overseas as quickly as possible. One of his superiors learned of the latest plans, and said, "Oh, no you don't. Indoctrination is mandatory." So Frank waited in Washington nearly three weeks for the next indoctrination session to begin, spent a few days undergoing the indoctrination, met our three children and me in New York on September 6, and on the 18th, we landed in Karachi. To wait. And wait.

To our amazement, we couldn't understand what the urgency was all about. While Frank waited for the Pakistanis to make a decision, he was put in charge of the Ganges Kopadek Dam and another big project in East Pakistan (1,000 miles away), and several smaller projects in West Pakistan.

The admiration and respect for Frank's work was reflected in his promotion in January 1954 to Project Advisor for all of East Pakistan (now Bangladesh). Four months later, in April 1954, he was promoted again to Assistant Chief of Water Resources, followed by a promotion to Chief of Water Resources nine months after that. He was now responsible for more than 10 major projects in East and West Pakistan, and served as Technical Supervisor of the division that was responsible for advising the planning, programming, implementation and execution of all types of reclamation, irrigation, power development, flood control and other engineering works that dealt with conservation, distribution and application of water resources in both East and West Pakistan. His work dealt primarily with building dams, constructing water conservation methods, telephones, sewers, and other projects that were critically important in a country as hot, dry and primitive as Pakistan was. As Chief of Water Resources, he served as the advisor to the Mission Director and top level Pakistan government and provincial officials.

Under the auspices of AID (Agency for International Development), one of his projects was that of helping to develop a conservative water system in the great Indus Valley, which upon completion, tripled Karachi's water supply.

Frank and many other government employees worked in Pakistan under very difficult circumstances while accomplishing a great deal to improve the country and the lives of the Pakistanis.

In the meantime, the children and I did what wives and children are supposed to do. We busied ourselves getting acquainted and learning about the country and its people. When we finally were able to get settled in our house, we were in a position to return many of the kindnesses that had been heaped upon us. In Karachi, we didn't invite someone over for a game of bridge, we invited them over for *dinner* and a game of bridge. When we first arrived, it was my intention to do all of the cooking. It didn't take me long to realize if I did all of the cooking, I would never crawl out of the kitchen. In fact, with the help (!) that we had those first few months, I could hardly ever escape from the kitchen as it was.

CHAPTER THIRTEEN

KARACHI SOCIAL LIFE UNBELIEVABLE

The heavy social life in Karachi was unbelievable. It should have been no surprise, however, because there was little else to do in the evenings and liquor (sans duty, but plus shipping charges of 30%) was almost as cheap as food. A liquor price list that Frank brought home read, in part:

1 case (12 bottles) Bellows Champagne or Sparkling
Burgundy----------------------------$10.00
1 case Crème de Menthe (De Kuyper) and Crème de
Cocoa---------------------------------$11.25 and $12.50
1 case Gilbey's Gin—$ 6.50
1 case Vodka (100 proof)—$11.60
1 case Bellows Scotch—$12.50
1 case Angus Scotch—$15.00
1 case Old Granddad Bourbon (100 proof)—$24.50
Cases of wine—$5.66—$10.41

I had always enjoyed entertaining but with the bearer we had working for us, it was really difficult. He was in low gear all of the time, but when I needed him to produce, he would come to a complete halt. I hadn't scolded him. Couldn't! There was something about his eyes resembling a St. Bernard's that kept me from doing so.

There seemed to be no end to cocktail parties, especially during the holidays, and by the end of January, they were still going strong. Two parties were particularly memorable. One was a huge reception given by the U.S. Ambassador to Pakistan Horace A. and Mrs. Hildreth in honor of Vice President and Mrs. Richard Nixon. The Nixons were delightful; wonderful representatives for the United States, we felt. The reception was strictly formal (as was everything after 6:30 p.m.), but this one was more elegant than usual. The guest list included all of the elite—dignitaries of every rank imaginable, including high-level government officials, ambassadors, attaches, generals, major generals, brigadier generals, admirals—the crème de la crème of Karachi society, dressed in formal attire, native dress, or military uniforms depicting rank or position. I had never seen so many dignitaries from the United States and foreign countries. They were all there to welcome our vice president and his lady. I was so proud of our honorees; so proud to be an American! The lump in my throat was so big that I was unable to speak for several seconds.

The other party to which I had been looking forward to was a formal dinner we had attended two nights earlier. It was hosted by Alhaj and Begum Mohammed Akram, our Pakistani friends, who were reputed to be the wealthiest people in Pakistan. Their mansion was truly Shangri La—and being a guest in it was an out of this world experience for both of us. Everything connected with it, from marble floors throughout the entire house, to the lovely tapestries, knick knacks, gorgeous figurines and lush Bokhara carpets, all of which had been imported from Italy, defied description.

As we entered the front door we faced a pair of circular marble stairs which gave a keyhole effect as they wound gracefully upwards to the second floor. The wall behind the staircase was entirely of glass brick, from floor to ceiling. The light fixture in the entrance hall was an enormous crystal chandelier which dangled from the ceiling, which must have been 30-feet high. Other light fixtures, shaped like clouds, were white and hung a few inches below the blue ceiling. The symbolism they imparted was that of clouds floating in a blue sky. The effect was spectacular and ethereal.

They also had an all-electric kitchen with every appliance available including a freezer, none of which they could use because there was not enough power. Their mansion, situated in the midst of tropical trees and foliage, seemed like a mirage in the desert, for beyond the grounds and the touches of man, the surrounding countryside was a barren wasteland of sand. This magnificent mansion was later sold (we were told) and became the Russian Embassy.

But that night we had entered the grounds past spectacular landscaping that surrounded an eight-foot marble goldfish bowl, also an Italian import. The guests, as impressive as the décor, included Prime Minister and Begum Mohammed Ali, several ambassadors including Horace and Mrs. Hildreth, and many other notables. The host and hostess were gracious and as appealing as their mansion. She was a lovely 5' 4" tall, clad in a sensational sari of pale blue Binari silk with silver thread design; he a dashing 6'5 ½", always handsome but especially so in his beautifully tailored tuxedo. They and their guests were delightful, and very appreciative of the help that America was giving them under the Foreign Aid Program.

At an earlier gathering, Alhaj told us that he made his fortune by buying up steel that the American military had strewn about on the Burma Road project and discarded after WWII. He then sold it on the black market, amassing a fortune in the process.

A few weeks before their big party, Begum Akram invited Frieda Thomas and me along with two other women to lunch so that we could see her collection of saris. At lunch we found ourselves dining at a 12-foot table of imported green onyx, inlaid with sterling silver shooting stars and signs of the zodiac. Following lunch, she led us down long marble hallways into her magnificent master bedroom. Dominating one wall were two enormous double beds side by side which were connected by a spectacular fan-shaped headboard of coral-colored tufted satin with built-in shelves on either side.

She unlocked her dressing room, which we discovered was larger than most of our living rooms. It was breathtaking! Six big closets, three on each of two walls, with mirrors and expensive wood inlay alternating on each door, were showcased. In each of these closets she had two racks crammed full of saris. She must have had a minimum of 50 saris on each rack, or 100 to a cupboard totaling a minimum of 600 saris of every imaginable color—almost all of the finest Binari silk and many with designs of pure gold or silver threads. Some of the saris that were trimmed with gold or silver were so heavy they had to be reinforced on the back. Some of the others were trimmed in zircons, or other stones; some with beads, and some with sequins. One closet was filled entirely with her wedding saris, over 100 of them—some given by tradition by the groom to his bride, others given by her family. The entire collection and the Shangri-La ambiance were awesome.

If Imelda Marcos of the Philippines had shoes, Begum Akram could probably have matched them two to one of every possible hue and design. On the way home one of the guests said, "Do you want to wipe the gold dust off of your hands and come in and see the formal I'm making out of a sheet?" We teased her about being an aristocrat for owning sheets.

We shared many pleasant experiences with the Akrams, one of which was a fishing trip on their magnificent yacht, which originally was a coastguard cutter. Doug, 10 years old at the time, was the champion fisherman that day, having bested the adults by catching five huge fish, out of a total of 11 fish caught! We brought Doug's fish home and placed them in the bathtub with water, not knowing where else to put them, and they promptly spoiled in the Pakistani heat. So much for that!

CHAPTER FOURTEEN

UNINVITED VISITOR

Joyce had been sick with a high fever, stomachache and headache for about a week, leading the Embassy nurse to think it might have been a light case of malaria. As Christmas approached, she was still pale and cranky so I took her to the hospital for tests and accidentally smashed her fingers in the car door when we returned home. The night before, a bus came within a cat's whisker of smashing into our car, and to top it off, our dachshund was in heat for the first time. I felt like writing to Dear Abby.

One morning, just a few days before Christmas, Judi rushed into my room and exclaimed excitedly, "Mother! There was a woman in my room!"

"A woman?"

"Yes, she had on a black burqua and a red dress and was looking under my bed!"

"You were probably dreaming, honey. What on earth would a woman be doing in your room?"

"I don't know, but she was there. It was so real, I couldn't have been dreaming. When I came out of the bathroom, she got up from the floor, said 'salaam' and hurried out of the room. I thought maybe she was a new sweeper."

I laughed and assured her that it was probably a dream. "It is possible, honey, but sometimes things seem to be so, when in reality they are merely figments of our imagination."

That seemed to satisfy her, but I wondered if there could have been someone in her room. Judi was a sensible child, not the imaginative type, and yet it was such a strange thing to dream about.

We went down to breakfast, but somewhat in doubt, I returned to the room that Judi and Joyce shared to get Joyce a dress, and casually looked around "just in case." I glanced out on the screen porch and walked through Doug's room. As I suspected, I saw nothing unusual. Judi felt sheepish by then, but insisted that she had not imagined it.

"I *wasn't* asleep," she insisted. "I had taken my shower and was coming out to comb my hair when there she was."

That's strange, I mused. If she had showered, surely she must have been awake.

Judi finished her breakfast and went upstairs, when suddenly she screamed. "Mother! There she is! There's that woman out in the yard! What'd I tell you? Look! A black burqua with red underneath!" Judi was shaking and crying by this time; terrified, but triumphant that she had been proven right!

The woman quickly slipped out of the gate. Doug and I followed in hot pursuit in time to see her turn into the gate next door. We called our bearer, who returned her to our compound for questioning. She was young—in her early 20s, probably—and rather attractive; dressed in a black burqua with a red sweater pinned underneath! One would never have suspected that she was a thief. She denied being in the house, lied without batting an eye, until the mali said he saw her both go into, and come out of, our house. She then showed us a letter which said they were Persian refugees without means of support—a standard ruse used by beggars to get money. We released her after deciding it would be more trouble than it was worth to call the police. However, we wished we had called them when we found evidence that she had been hiding in Doug's closet, and apparently had been in the house for nearly an hour before Judi discovered her trying to get under her bed. Luckily, the bed was too low.

Later we learned from the bearer next door that there were three women working the houses together; two young ones, and an older one with a gold front tooth. Two hours later when the woman with the gold tooth came to our door with a typewritten slip attesting to being the wife of a Palestinian refugee with 10 children to support, I took her paper to my desk and wrote across it in ink, "This woman is a thief!" folded it up, and told our bearer to give it back to her. I had hoped the warning might help someone before she discovered the note was on the slip. Sure enough, Jeannie, one of Judi's classmates, told about returning to their house later that day and finding the same woman inside. No one knew how she entered because all of the doors were locked. Jeannie said, "When we asked her what she was doing there, she handed us a paper on which somebody had written in ink "This woman is a thief." When Jeannie's mother learned that I was the one who had written the note she thanked me for the warning and told me that it took three of her servants to force her out of the house. Later we heard that two of the thieves had been arrested by the police, flogged, and released to continue preying upon the unsuspecting.

The most glorious event of the past year was the fabulous and colorful Platinum Jubilee celebration of His Royal Highness the Aga Khan when he was weighed against platinum at the Aga Khan Gymkhana Karachi on February 3, 1954. Unfortunately, we were not able to get tickets to attend the event, but Joyce and I went back the next day and sat in the seat upon which the Aga sat when he was weighed, hoping some of his wealth would rub off on us! (It hasn't yet!) Later we drove around past the house where he was born, which was located two or three miles from our house. The house, trees, and most of the grounds were ablaze with a profusion of sparkling yellow lights. Spectacular. Where did *they* get the power, we wondered?

According to *DAWN*, Karachi's English language newspaper, the celebration took place before a select gathering of almost 50,000 dignitaries from all corners of the globe at a specially erected amphitheater "to witness this paragon of glory". The Karachi site of the Platinum Jubilee celebration was significant because Karachi had the distinction of being the birthplace of His Royal Highness.

Earlier, HRH had been weighed against gold at the Golden Jubilee Celebration in 1936, and against diamonds at the Diamond Jubilee Celebration in 1946. Both events were held in Bombay, marking 50 and 60 years respectively, as Imam of the Ismailis. Proceeds from the Golden and Diamond Jubilee celebrations were donated to the organization of schools, clinics, dispensaries, child-welfare centers and education for the Ismaili community. Proceeds from the Platinum Jubilee, in honor of the Prince's 70 years of his imamate, were donated by His Highness for the establishment of an industrial finance corporation for the Ismaili sect.

Two days following the Platinum Jubilee celebration—at 9:45 a.m. on Friday, February 5, 1954—we were at the pier with the school children and the entire American community watching the flagship U.S.S. Pittsburgh, commanded by Vice-Admiral Jerauld Wright, Commander-in-Chief of

U.S. Naval Forces in Eastern Atlantic and Mediterranean, pull into port. Every once in awhile, Doug had the uncanny ability to make some choice remark. This day was no exception. The sailors were all lined up on the deck of the heavy cruiser in their dress whites, standing at attention as the 21-gun salute sounded off. The HMPS 'Qasim,' Manora Shore Battery, returned the 21-gun salute. It was then so quiet you could have heard the proverbial pin drop. Doug yelled out, "Hey, I don't think you guys will like it here. Here everything is done by hand!"

The sailors broke all regulations and burst into a guffaw that could have been heard all the way to India and back!

I grabbed Doug by the arm. All the way to the car he kept dragging his feet saying, "Gee, Mom! What'd I say, Mom; what'd I say? Ah Geeeeeeez!" He was 23 years old before I finally explained to him the inference of his statement.

I threatened the kids with their lives if they revealed who had made that remark when we had four sailors to dinner the next day. Our guests represented Oregon, Washington, Massachusetts and Pittsburgh—none from Colorado to our disappointment. They were all delightful, however, as were others whom we helped entertain at the Ambassador's residence the following night. Along with meeting such fine young men stationed so far from home, we were able to buy 5 pounds of pork, a big piece of cheese, and a hunk of salami from their ship. And no one mentioned Doug's classic remark—thank goodness!

CHAPTER FIFTEEN

LOCAL SCENES AND CUSTOMS

A friend was telling us that he had recently gone partridge shooting in the innermost part of the Northwestern Province and he said "natives came out of the woodwork" to shake his hand and through interpreters, tell him how grateful they were for the American Aid they were receiving. The overall consensus was that the "U.S. has rendered the nation invaluable economic, technical and military aid."

Activities that American children enjoyed in Pakistan were very similar to those they would have enjoyed in the States, with exceptions that were flavored with local scenes and customs such as birthday parties that consisted of dancing monkeys, snake charmers with cobras, turtle hunts and rides on donkey carts.

One day I took Judi and some other children to a tennis lesson and got hopelessly lost trying to get home.

We enjoyed the first hour because we were seeing parts of Karachi we had never seen before. The second hour was another story. I approached taxi drivers, policemen and pedestrians—everybody who looked as though they might know some English. I asked them if they could direct us to the American Embassy, but they didn't understand. I learned later that if I had said, "Am reek an Embossy" instead of American Embassy, they would have known where we wanted to go. How we finally found our way home, I'll never know. It just happened.

Our treks through the city and the bazaars were always interesting experiences. One of our favorite finds was a sidewalk "dentest."

Although there were a number of sidewalk dentists, this one was unique because tacked to a nearby tree was one sign in English that read "DENTEST," plus a second sign in Urdu (the official Pakistani language). Tethered to the same tree were two fat-tailed rams, and not two feet away on the other side of the tree were his equipment, medicine, and false teeth laid out in a neat row on a dirty cloth. Nearby was a quarter of a bushel basket filled with teeth that he apparently had extracted. I had just finished taking his picture when a patient plopped into the chair. The "dentest" picked up the mirrored instrument that they use, wiped it on his filthy shirt tail, and stuck it into the patient's mouth. Using a foot-operated drill, he began working on the man's tooth. We didn't wait to see the result.

Across the street from the "dentest" was a Karachi version of the medicine man, sitting cross legged on the sidewalk, sharing a "hookah pipe" (used to smoke tobacco and/or opium) with two other fellows. Such an assortment of herbs, bugs, snakes and spiders (most of them preserved in jars) as that man had! He also had a few extracted teeth on display, along with a rusty pair of pliers, but the teeth didn't impress us half as much as the dishpan full—heaping full—of dead lizards with all kinds of red juice oozing out of them. We learned by sign language that they were just the thing to cure rheumatism, sciatica, and whatever else might ail you! After looking at them, then looking at a cage full of live lizards that were stacked about four deep in their cage, we decided we didn't want to know what they were for. We had had enough of the local medical profession for one day.

Bunderboating was one of the favorite pastimes of people in Karachi. A bunderboat resembled a large sailboat, the difference being the bunder which was a large, heavy plank that small, bronzed natives threw from side to side in order to balance the boat as it tipped. They quickly tucked the bunder under a big rope to hold it firm, and then from two to four natives scampered upon the bunder, squatting to steady the boat. Our first experience was relatively calm and a lot of fun; the second experience was another story. It was a terribly windy day and those poor fellows slammed the bunder around as though it were a match stick, from side to side, then rushed up to squat on it before the boat tipped over. Doug had the time of his life riding the bunders with the natives, and watching the seamen as they scrambled up the rope like monkeys when they hoisted the brownish, dirty, sail. Because the sail was patched in a number of places, and because we were on a wild, bouncing ride, I held my breath and hoped the natives would succeed. None of us wanted to repeat that performance.

Being novices that we were, we planned to have a picnic on the beach after our bunderboat ride. No packed lunch for us. No Siree! We would barbecue hamburgers on the beach. I baked some buns and fried up some potato chips, made potato salad and a chocolate cake. We ground the beef and made patties ahead of time. At the beach we barbecued the meat on a charcoal broiler that our friends brought along. The thing we hadn't counted on was the wind—a 40-mile gale that blasted sand over every mouthful of food that we tried to eat. We wiped off the dishes; wiped out the glasses, and before we could get a drink or put food on our plates, they would be blanketed with sand again. The potato salad, chocolate cake, and hamburgers were all well seasoned with sand, and so was the beer! Before we were through spitting sand, we had attracted a slew of natives, camels, and dogs, not to mention huge birds that swooped down and tried to steal the food right off of our plates.

Meanwhile, at the Crazy House, things were beginning to settle down. One day, a carpenter was there building shelves; the mali had just come in to fill the water tank (which was on the roof and the only access was up the 47 steps that were inside the house); I had just shooed off a door-to-door walla, and the hamal came in and asked if I would like to have a cup of coffee.

"I'd love to have a cup of coffee," I said.

"No? O.K. I go make food," and out he went. I had learned another lesson. If I had answered a simple 'yes', I would have been served coffee.

Many days the confusion reminded me of Grand Central Station. February 8 was a typical day. There were six fellows installing our one and only air conditioner in the bedroom; the sweeper was in and out emptying garbage; the plumber was working with four helpers in the bathroom; the hamal and bearer were watching everyone else work to see that nothing was stolen; the dhobi was washing and ironing; the carpenter was on hand to do odd jobs around the house; the kids were fighting, and I was ready to lose my mind with all of the traffic, pounding and hammering that was going on. Before the day was over, I was ready to climb the walls. "It won't be the 'E*gg and I'* when I write my book," I decided. "It will be '*Down the Drain with Jane*'."

I was reminded of the story one of our neighbors told about a pregnant friend of hers who had three bathrooms in her house, but on one occasion tore through Dana's house to use one of her bathrooms because she figured it was quicker to zip in there than to wait for her own help to get through cleaning her bathrooms! That's the best way I could describe the speed with which many of those people worked. It was fascinating to watch artisans at work. For example, the carpenter. He sat on the floor and held the wood he was working on with the soles of his feet instead of his hands. He then chiseled holes in the walls and filled the holes with scraps of wood to hold the nails securely. Great solution!

The plumbing was an endless problem in the Crazy House, especially the pipes in the master bathroom which were always leaking. The regular ritual was to call the American Embassy and request the plumber. That meant a trip down a block and over one, stepping cautiously over piles of camel dung, to reach the nearest telephone. In due time, a little pock-faced, bow-legged man would appear, carrying a dingy bag that held his tools. He would totter before me, this man of indefinite age, and grin a toothy grin dripping with beetle juice that had years ago stained his teeth a rusty red, and make his way without direction to the faulty sink. His clothes were tattered and had lost their white when they were new at Ramazan some months before. Instead of the voluminous shalwar trousers worn by most Pakistanis, he was covered, but barely, in filthy shorts of the sweeper class and with a dirty turban that usually covered his hair and half of one eye.

Tools! That was a matter of opinion we thought as he took out a ball of twine and wrapped it carefully around the leaking pipe, and painted the twine with aluminum paint. Invariably, he would put his 'tools' away, bow down low with the beetle juice dripping out of the spaces where his teeth had been; draw himself up to his full 4'5", and, as he tottered down the stairs, wave gaily yelling, "Feexed, Mem Sahib. Feexed!" Until tomorrow, that was!

Our friend, George Thomas, related an experience he had had with an electrician the Embassy had sent over to fix his refrigerator.

"He had a long piece of wire, but made a mistake and cut it too short, so he draped it across the kitchen door. Anyone wishing to go through the door had to crawl on his hands and knees to get through. He 'fixed' the refrigerator by brushing some paint on a gas leak in the motor. During the time that he was there, he put a coat of paint over the leak, sat and waited for it to dry; applied another coat, waited some more, and kept repeating the process for eight hours," George explained.

"I was fit to be tied," George said. "I threw the paint can out, and slammed the refrigerator door. The 'electrician' almost had a fit!"

"No, Sahib! No! Have to close door quiet. If slam, it stop working!"

George was furious by now, and slammed the door repeatedly, at least 10 times. The electrician, begging him to use care, said "No, Sahib! No! It quit, Sahib. It quit!"

Sure enough it did, which is exactly what George wanted it to do.

"If the refrigerator quits by slamming the door, it is *not* working right!" George yelled.

George told us about a friend of his who had a gun with powder in it, so he told his bearer to build a fire in the back yard and burn the powder out. Instead, the bearer held the gun over the kitchen sink.

Now it seems as though their sink is no longer water proof, what with two big holes in the basin!

I hired a derzee (tailor) to make a formal for me out of some yellow net that I had brought from the States, only to discover that he had stolen almost all of my thread while he was there (my two-year supply!) I had been careful to bring thread to match all of the fabric that I brought to Pakistan, and now it was gone. I refused to go out and buy more yellow thread, instead insisted that he finish the dress with white thread, but the overall result wasn't as good as it should have been. Since labor was fairly cheap in Karachi, I intended to have most of my own clothes made, but planned to sew the children's clothes myself. I planned to get a new derzee, too!

CHAPTER SIXTEEN

HE DIDN'T KNOW THE GUN WAS LOADED

1995 started out with a bang, and I mean that literally! On January 2, our 10-year-old son raced into the house and burst into hysterics. "Mother," he screamed. "I shot Gil with his .22!"

We jumped from our chairs. "*YOU WHAT*!"

"I just shot Gil in the stomach. Oh, Mother, I didn't mean to do it! Honest I didn't! I didn't know the gun was loaded. Honest, I didn't! Oh, is he going to die? Is he?" He was crying uncontrollably and trembling so badly that it took us a few seconds to find out what had happened.

"I don't think it's real bad," he blurted. "It hit his arm and then went into his side"—he pointed to an area above the appendix region—" but not very deep. (This was almost a prayer). "They think they can feel the bullet, and it's only in about an inch!"

Frank was sobbing and Doug was pulling at my dress, screaming, "Spank me hard, Mother—Oh, please *SPANK ME HARD—SPANK ME HARD!*"

"Stop it, Doug," I demanded. "*STOP IT*!" I was shaking him by the shoulders now. "Snap out of it! This is serious. Acting this way won't help matters at all. We've got to get to the hospital, and get there *FAST*!"

He quieted down somewhat and pleaded to go to the hospital with us. I knew he wanted to know the details as soon as we could learn them, so I agreed, providing he stayed in the car until we knew more.

I felt sorry for Gil and his family, but my heart bled for Doug, too. Hell itself couldn't compare with the agony that child was going through.

He was terribly in the wrong. He had been around guns enough that he should have known to check to see if it was loaded, but he had failed to do so. How costly would this mistake be? My knees were shaking. Silently, I prayed that it would work out all right.

Frank was so upset that there was no way he could have driven. Because I habitually drove faster than he did, I knew I could get to the hospital quicker than he could have anyway. Grabbing the steering wheel, I raced to the hospital through heavy bicycle traffic, arriving within minutes with Frank and Doug moaning beside me.

Anxiously, we asked at the desk if Gil had been admitted there, and to our surprise the attendant said, "No. I've been here since 2:00 p.m. and no such case has come in. I glanced at my watch. It was now 5:10 p.m. The shooting took place about 4:45 p.m.; Doug reached home about 5:00 p.m. Tony, a friend of Gil's family, was also waiting, and had alerted the X-ray department and operating rooms to stand by pending the boy's arrival. Because Gil's religion was Catholic, we called a nearby Catholic maternity hospital to make sure he hadn't gone there. They might have taken emergency patients, and we had to be sure. "No such case," they told us, so we paced up and down the sidewalk watching for Gil's family car. The minutes dragged by like hours and still no sign of them. Three times we called the maternity hospital; three times they told us no such case had been admitted.

Three little beggars came to us demanding bachsheas (money). I wanted to scream and claw at them. Couldn't they see we were upset? Didn't they know it might well be a matter of life and death? Of course they didn't, poor wretched souls. How could they know; how could they care?

Then Tony called Gil's house and was informed by their bearer that Gil's parents had left some minutes before with Gil. He added that Gil was then unconscious. Doug shivered and started to cry again. Silently I prayed. Frank had been mumbling prayers from his rosary, and to Doug, I said, "Listen son, if you've never prayed before in your life, you'd better do it now!"

"Yeah, Mom," and he disappeared into the car and down on his knees out of sight.

Still the minutes dragged on. Had they been in an accident? Had they gone to another hospital? That was doubtful because the Seventh-Day Adventist Hospital was the principal one in the city. Had he not survived the trip to the hospital? I shivered at the thought. Suddenly, the family's driver drove in front of the hospital. My heart sank. There was nothing but the driver and a pillow in the car! My first fear was that he had not survived, but I was wrong.

"He's not in danger," the driver said, clasping his hands in front of him in a prayer-like fashion. "He's at the Catholic Hospital. He has been X-rayed and his doctors say he will be all right!"

"Thank you, dear God!" I said. Doug fell to his knees. I covered my mouth to suppress a scream. Frank looked like a ghost. We were all crying tears of relief. Tony, the family friend, ordered, "Follow me!" We each made a U turn in the middle of Bunder Road, bringing the heavy traffic to a screeching halt, and sped over to the other hospital. Gils's family was much calmer than we were. Inadequate as words were at a time like that, I tried to express my condolences; to tell them how terribly sorry we were that our boy had injured their son.

"Forget it!" Gil's father said simply, without any sign of anger. "It could just as easily have been the other way around."

Rory, their four-year-old, tugged at his mother's skirt and said, "Guess some of it's my fault, Mummy. I loaded the bullet in."

Gil, the 10-year-old son of a *New York Times* reporter, had been given a .22 rifle and bullets for a Christmas present by his parents! Even though there were six children in the family, four of them 4½-years of age and under, the gun was left within their reach, and the 4½-year-old boy had inserted the bullet. Doug, not knowing it was loaded, picked up the gun, aimed it at the wall, and pulled the trigger just as Gil emerged from the bathroom. The family informed us later that apparently Gil's belt buckle had deflected the bullet, he had never been unconscious, nor had he been in pain at any time except where the bullet had scraped his arm. The X-rays didn't show the bullet, but his doctor kept him in the hospital overnight in case anything unforeseen developed.

Gil was pale, but quipping "Good, now I don't have to go to school for awhile. I can't read—see, my arm's bandaged."

We were all tremendously relieved, and it was a much wiser boy who was discharged from the hospital the next day. It was clear that Gil felt much better than Doug did. Doug had been sick to his stomach all night and the next day from the shock.

Sorry as we were that Gil had been injured, I was furious at the family for being so careless as to leave a gun and bullets in the reach of small children! I was sure Doug had learned his lesson; my hope was that Gil's family had learned their lesson as well.

CHAPTER SEVENTEEN

ISLAMIC RELIGION RULES PAKISTANIS

The longer we remained in Pakistan, the more apparent it became how much the religion dominated the life of the Muslims. The Islamic religion and life are inseparable to these people. They are face to face with God at all times. It was not simply a religion; it was (and is) a way of life.

According to lore, the Islamic religion was founded by Mohammed in the year 609 A.D. when, at the age of 40, he became known as the Messenger of God after the archangel Gabriel commanded him in a vision to read.

"I cannot read," he responded.

"Read!"

"I cannot!"

The third time Mohammed was ordered to read, he read the words of God and is said to have told his begum (wife) later, "The words remained as though inscribed on my heart."

Islam is the youngest of the great religions and one-seventh of the world's population has been converted to its doctrines. It is one of the simplest and most explicit of religions, believing in one God and in the brotherhood of man, regardless of race or skin color. The key to its success has been its policy regarding brotherhood, and the key to its power is to be found in the word "Islam" which to the devout means complete submission of body and soul to the will of God. They believe that Jesus was a prophet, not the son of God. And they believe Mohammed was not only a speaker for God, but that he was the last and greatest prophet of all.

Mohammed made the laws of the Old Testament the foundation for his teachings, and although he established neither priesthood nor sacraments, his teachings represent to the Muslims the final and absolute word of God.

I read all that I could about the Muslim religion because to understand their religion was to understand the Pakistanis—or at least it helped. I read the Koran, the Islamic scriptures, noting that among many rules for correct conduct, were the five main tenets as decreed by Mohammed. Known as the "Five Pillars of Islam," they are:

1) There is no God but Allah; Mohammed is the Messenger of Allah;
2) Prayers must be performed facing Mecca, his birthplace, five times a day wherever one is, and in the mosques on Fridays;
3) Almsgiving must be given as an offering to Allah;
4) Believers must undergo Ramazan, a month of fasting, in order to obtain a more perfect communion with God;
5) All followers must make a pilgrimage to Mecca during their lifetime.

Mohammed's followers carefully wrote down his teachings on anything that was available such as palm leaves or the dried skin and bones of sheep. The Koran, which is said to have been compiled by one of Mohammed's secretaries after his death, is said to contain the teachings of God as transmitted to Mohammed. It contains many laws of behavior and practices; forbids the use of pork or alcohol in any form; forbids gambling and usury; raised the status of women from that of mere animalism to, if not equality to man, a semblance of it; and gave men permission to marry four wives at one time—i.e. ". . . marry of the women who seem good to you, two or three or four; and if ye fear that ye cannot do justice to so many, then one only . . ."

The power of divorce was given to the husband, and not to the wife, except in rare cases. When a man divorces, all he has to do is clap his hands four times, declaring each time that he does not wish to have this woman and the divorce is finalized.

Of special interest to us was that the poor Pakistanis were much stricter about adhering to the rules of the Islamic religion, than were the upper class. Many (but not all) of the people with whom we associated socially ate pork, drank cocktails and violated other rules of Islamic behavior, whereas the destitute and blue-collar workers were almost always strict adherents. For example, we once invited our first bearer, Shafi, to have a glass of Coca-Cola.

"No, Madam," he said.

"Why not, Shafi?" I said. "There is nothing in Coca-Cola that violates your religion."

"I know, Madam. But maybe it is in the refrigerator, and maybe there is bacon there."

"But. Shafi," I argued. "Coca-Cola is in a bottle, and the bacon can't contaminate it."

"No, Madam. Book say no," he responded stubbornly.

The fast of Ramazan is calculated by the position of the moon. When an appointed watcher observes a thin slip of silver above the sunken sun's brightness, he sends his message: The fasting month's moon, the Horned Moon of Islam, had been seen. The fast begins and lasts for an entire month at the hottest time of the year.

During this time the Muslim abstains from all food and drink between sunrise and sunset, even refraining from frivolities, smoking or sex. The purpose of Ramazan is for the Muslims to condition themselves for such time as they are forced to do without, either through poverty, wartime, or other hardships.

Both of our servants observed the fast, which meant that they had to rise at a given hour, "Sehri" [from three to four a.m., depending on when dawn breaks through,] and were told the exact minute they could eat. They then had to go through the entire day without food, water or any other liquids, during this miserably hot period until the Muezzin [the man who called people to prayer] rang a bell at sunset announcing "iftar".

For instance, the first time we experienced Ramazan was in June, 1954, with Sehri at 4:14 a.m., and Iftar at 7:17 p.m. After the bell rang at night they could eat all they wished before the bell rang announcing Sehri, but nothing in between. We were warned to expect servants to act strangely, woe-be-gone, with shorter tempers, and accomplish little or nothing during the month of fast. We were also told to be prepared to give them bonuses at the end of the fast during which there is usually a three-day celebration akin to Christian Christmas celebrations. At the end of the fast, everybody who possibly could was decked out in fresh, white clothing.

One day, we experienced the depth of their religious observance when we asked Aziz what had happened to some cigarettes. He was deeply offended, and quit on the spot, because he thought we were accusing him of taking them.

"We're not accusing you, Aziz. Mem Sahib would merely like to know because we don't know who has them, it might even be the children," Frank said.

After explanations were made and clarified on each side, we hired him back. One of my neighbor's servants told my neighbor, "I knew Mem Sahib [me] take him back. They right for each other!"

Dealing with Aziz was as tricky as if we were taking back a wayward offspring. I made every effort to forget the incident ever happened, but it was difficult because he was so sensitive. I always felt as though I were treading on thin ice.

We tried several times to give him cigarettes after that happened. The last time was one day when I was decorating the house for Christmas, I offered him two packages of cigarettes as a thank you for conducting a successful dinner party, but he refused. I was crushed, and asked him not to feel that way about it.

"Forget what happened, Aziz. I've forgotten."

He nervously wrung his hands and smiled sheepishly, shuffled first on one foot and then on the other before saying,

"Scuse me, please, Madam. I give promise to God"—and with that he pulled on both of his ear lobes [a sign of complete submission and repentance]—"that I never touch no more cigarettes."

"Oh, but this is different; this is a gift. Please accept them, Aziz."

"Scuse me, please, Madam. I promise never no more cigarettes."

"You mean you've quit smoking?" I was astounded.

"No, Madam. Just never no more American cigarettes."

My Christmas spirit went into a tailspin right then. I asked him if he couldn't change the rules or something, but one look at his face convinced me that no amount of persuasion would do any good. He had made his promise to Allah, and that was final.

The main holidays, which included celebrating August fourteenth as Pakistani Independence Day, were no sooner finished than we began planning a trip to India by car—an almost unheard of thing to do.

Arranging details took the better part of the summer, interrupted only by Joyce's fourth birthday celebration on August thirty-first.

Unlike children's birthday parties in the states, her party was uniquely Pakistani. Our cook/bearer located a street walla who came to our house at the appointed time with his trained monkeys, a large pot in which a cobra was coiled, and an instrument that resembled a flute. The snake charmer squatted cross-legged on the ground wearing dirty shalwar pants and a kamiz (long knee-length shirt worn loosely over the pants.) A dirty, ill-fitting turban, wound haphazardly around his head, completed his ensemble. As he played some tunes, the monkeys danced in circles and cavorted around wildly until he caged them.

The snake charmer then began playing some eerie-sounding melodies, spinning the flute around in circles, slowly at first, then faster and faster. As he did so, the snake's head began rising out of the pot, undulating to the beat of the music. We were glad we were sitting safely out of his reach, and breathed sighs of relief when the snake charmer left the premises. After the entertainment, Aziz served the children a beautiful home-made cake and lemonade to their delight.

When September 4, 1954, rolled around four days later, we were packed and on our way to India—for the adventure of our lives!

Amir, the waiter at the Beach Luxury Hotel, Karachi, was so devoted to Joyce that he was frequently punished for leaving his station and moving to ours so that he could feed her. He is shown with Joyce and Judi.

Our first house was dubbed the Crazy House because of its unusual construction. Two-thirds of the house, which was our portion, had 14 rooms. There were three large bedrooms, each with baths; two kitchens; a breakfast room; a giant-sized dining room; an enormous living room; a fruit room; a storage room; and a large screened-in porch that connected two of the bedrooms.

A scene from a Moharram Day parade, showing the crowds of observers and a tazia in the distance. A tazia is a replica of a tomb constructed by different guilds; for example, a tazia made entirely of bangles would be built by the bangle guild; a tazia of cotton weavers would be made entirely of cotton and be built by the cotton guild, and so forth.

Close-up of a tazia. The tazias were carried the length of the Moharram Day parade and submerged in the river to drown the evil spirits.

The author on camel back.

Our son, Doug, at the beach with a baby camel.

Joyce with our cook/bearer, Aziz.

The Tessitor family outfitted in typical Pakistani costumes.

A durzee (tailor) shown sitting on our terrazzo-tile floor, spinning with his hand the wheel of a Singer sewing machine that had no table and no legs.

Azim, our mali (gardener). He was no fashion plate, but he won the prize for being our most devoted servant.

A sample of the onlookers that followed us wherever we went. We eventually learned that the natives followed us in droves because they thought Joyce, with her platinum blond hair, was a gift from Allah.

Joyce covering her head with a bedspread. She was pretending she was in "purdah" like the Pakistani women.

The Governor's elite bodyguards frequently invited us to mounted displays which they held on important occasions such as when they were hosting visiting dignitaries. The exhibitions consisted of musical rides, the Governor General's carriage with postillions in full dress, individual horsemanship exhibitions, show jumping, tent pegging on horseback, wrestling on horseback, relay racing, and other events

One of the elaborate mosques in Agra, India.

Joyce, Doug, and Judi Tessitor (from left) dressed in Pakistani costumes.

Joyce Tessitor posing on her fourth birthday.

A donkey cart, driven by Doug, and filled with children who were celebrating Joyce's fourth birthday.

The author posing on the sands by the Arabian Sea.

Crocodiles (considered sacred) in the town of Mohangapir, near Karachi.

Suzie, the huge sea turtle that we captured, named and brought to our house in Karachi. Feeling sorry for her, we returned her to the ocean two days later. When she was freed, she raised her head, sniffed the ocean, and rapidly disappeared under a wave.

Another scene from Joyce's fourth birthday party. Our mali (gardener) often made her floral houses and gardens out of sun-baked mud. One of them is shown, along with Mohammed, our bearer, and our mali (back row); Joyce and her friends (front row).

Mohammed, our bearer, carrying Joyce.

Outdoor barber shop in a refugee camp. Dentists, food stands, barber shops, and similar businesses were conducted on sidewalks all over the city

Fortune teller, Karachi. One of numerous businesses that flourished on the streets.

Joyce "shopping" in a Karachi bazaar.

Gentlemen, at the airport, dressed in lunghies. A back view shows how they draped the five yards of material to form their "trousers."

Back view of burquas. Six yards of material were fashioned like this in the back. The fronts were draped similarly with the entire face covered, except the eyes. They were covered with a crochet-like fabric from which the ladies could see, but would not be seen.

Natives at an outdoor drinking fountain.

The famous Red Fort in Lahore, Pakistan, at which hundreds of sacred monkeys cavorted around.

Bird man, another street business, in Agra, India.

Straw huts in a refugee camp, Karachi.

A funeral procession in Karachi.

A herd of goats, typical of those that frequently stopped traffic.

Children in East Pakistan. The boy (on the right) is wearing a lunghy; the small child in the center is naked except for a small bell or trinket that is placed on him (or her) at birth to ward off the evil spirits. They wear this trinket until they die.

The Tessitor family with the Taj Mahal, Agra, in the background.

The Tessitor children with Aziz, our cook/bearer. The Taj Mahal is in the background.

A submerged car is an example of the damage that was done from the Lahore flood that we experienced. The rainstorm, unprecedented in Lahore history, rained 15.34 inches in 33 hours, most of it during the first 12 hours.

Further damage from the Lahore flood.

The day after the flood, showing natives fleeing into the unknown. Hundreds of natives lost their huts and all of their belongings. Devastation was everywhere.

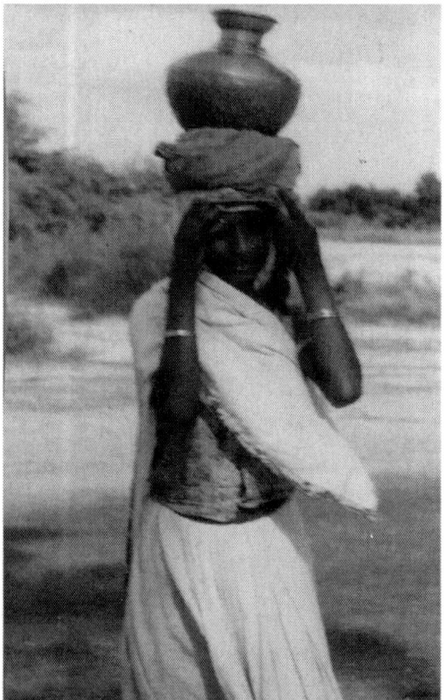

An Indian coolie walking down the road on the outskirts of Agra with a water jug on her head.

A mosque at the Red Fort in Multan, Pakistan.

Our friend, engineer, and artist, Ismaili, painted this portrait of our 10-year-old son, Doug, with a palette knife. It is an excellent likeness, and one of my fondest treasures.

A portrait of our cook/bearer Aziz, painted from life by the author. It is a superb likeness of our best servant who was so temperamental that we finally had to let him go.

A portrait of the Governor General's bodyguards. The author painted this portrait by looking at a picture that was printed in a magazine. It is an accurate depiction of the guards and their uniforms.

The Tessitor children dressed for the return home.

Jane Tessitor Braun and Mai Tai, her silky terrier.

CHAPTER EIGHTEEN

TEST CASE

Never in my wildest dreams did I imagine we would have had such a variety of experiences during our stint in Pakistan—some humorous, some pleasant, some not so pleasant, but all of them had been interesting. Now that the end of our tour was coming to a close, I was spending an inordinate amount of time vacillating between plans for our next 11 months and wondering how we could accomplish all of the things we wanted to do during our remaining tour.

The climate, however, was beginning to take its toll, and we no longer had the pep or enthusiasm that we once had. It was obvious that we needed a change; something had to be done. So, during the summer of 1954, we proceeded to develop plans for driving 3,500 miles from Karachi to parts of India. Officials at AID (Agency for International Development) were not against the idea, but knew of no other Americans undertaking such a trip by car. When we applied for clearance to take our car across the Indian border we were told our trip would be a test case. We spent a lot of time asking the advice of Pakistanis and others who were familiar with the territory, and decided to give it a try. We opted to take Aziz on the trip with us partly as a thank-you for doing such a fine job for us as cook/bearer; partly because we thought he would be a valuable interpreter. We thought we would be doing him a favor; little did we realize how invaluable he would be for us!

The hurdles that we encountered in the planning stages made us wonder if we were out of our minds. Would the roads be passable? Would we be able to get petrol (gas) when we needed it? What about accommodations?

What about food ? When we were in remote areas, would we be able to find food that we could eat?

Aziz quickly allayed our fears.

"No worry, Madam. I find food." He never failed us.

Regarding accommodations, our worries were dispelled when we were informed that the Government of Pakistan had some good rest houses in almost every city that we would be visiting. We proceeded to make reservations in those places, and began applying for visas to India for our family and a passport and visa for our cook/bearer. We then began the complicated arrangements for the necessary clearance to get our car through the heavily guarded Indian border.

Finally, the day of our departure arrived. After packing provisions, bedding, extra gas, kids and our cook/bearer, we started out. What could be sweeter than to start on a camping trip and bring a servant along to do the work? Let's get this straight right now—without him I would have headed for home after our first meal out. It was September 4, and the 114-degree heat that we experienced the first day was unmerciful. There was no air conditioning in the car. We were not sweltering; we were roasting! The scenery was filtered through shimmering heat waves as we "sped" over corrugated ruts at a maximum speed of 30 miles per hour for mile after mile. Oh, God, I thought to myself. Was this a portent of the entire trip?

In an attempt to cool off, we soaked some towels in water and draped them over all of the windows except those that Frank, as driver, needed to see out of. The wet towels didn't help much. In the distance we could see one tree miles away. We hungered for its shade.

"My nose feels dry, but its dripping," Judi groaned. "My throat is scratchy; my lips are parched; my skin is clammy." By the time we stopped at the very lovely government rest house in Sukker, I was sick to my stomach and Judi said she wished she were dead. We had been driving through almost nothing but dusty, barren country for hours and hours, and oh, how I wished we could go back and wait until December to try it. The thought of repeating that part of the trip sounded terrible and since all reservations were made, there was nothing to do but to continue. Thank goodness for Aziz. I never could have taken care of the family that night. He lugged our baggage, provisions and bedding up umpteen flights of stairs, fixed the beds, cooked dinner, washed dishes, boiled water for drinking, made arrangements for tea, and did the many other odd jobs that had to be done.

The Sukker Rest House, a Pakistani government-sponsored inn, far exceeded our expectations. It was as attractive, or more so, than many residential hotels we had seen in our own country. The spacious lawns were beautifully landscaped; there were numerous rooms (I never did get around to counting them all), but those that we examined were spotlessly clean. Accommodations were pleasant. All of this was for the asking. The bottom line was that it cost us a couple of rupees for tips to each of the servants and that was it! We would have liked to spend the balance of our vacation right there. But, it was not to be. *We had a trip to take care of. We were going to India!*

Refreshed, but not eager, we left our comfortable surroundings, the next morning and made our way across the Sukker Barrage, which was an artificial dam that was constructed to divert water for irrigation. Then we traveled up into the Sindhi country, the home of the Sindhi tribes, en route to Multan where we had our next reservations.

We passed innumerable herds of buffalo, goats, and sheep, as well as countless natives trudging up the road on foot or riding on donkey or camel back. We saw very few women. Occasionally, alongside the roads, we would see them, but seldom in the villages, for idling in public was a luxury afforded the men only. We passed through several of those little villages, each one dusty and dirty with bazaars on either side of the road where the men would congregate to gossip and share their hookah pipes with their friends. Once in awhile, a man would trot by carrying straw or something else on his head or his back.

The next morning, after Aziz fixed a nice breakfast in the rest house kitchen and re-packed all of our things, we headed for Multan. This part of the trip, scenically, was quite pleasant. The country was much greener; desert, yes, but lots of big trees covered each side of much of the road and clumps of tall saw grass were scattered throughout the desert. We passed many tribes of Sindhi nomads (which appeared to be entire families) on their trek to more lucrative surroundings. Some were journeying on foot; others were riding camels; still others were riding miniature donkeys with their meager belongings fastened to the backs of the animals. The donkeys were so small that the feet of the riders were almost touching the ground. We passed a lot of rice paddies; saw many little straw and mud huts with curved roofs, nestled in groves of date palms, and stopped frequently during the day to take pictures of the countryside and its people. We took movies of several nomads traveling up the road with their donkeys laden high with bundles of sticks; took a shot of a rooster crowing from atop a donkey's back, photographed a mother nursing her baby while she traveled on donkey back, and took a lot of pictures of natives plowing fields with oxen while using the most primitive of implements.

"Gosh, their heads must be strong," Doug said as we watched woman after woman trudging barefooted down the road with huge loads of straw on their heads.

Everywhere we drove, the natives would stop their work and stare awestruck at our car. Cars were not unheard of, but were surely a novelty, and the roads were surprisingly good, although not up to our standards by any means.

CHAPTER NINETEEN

MULTAN: HEAT HAZE, SAND AND BUZZARDS

We finally reached Multan about 4:00 that afternoon, parched, tired and hungry. It is said to be the hottest point in Pakistan, and we weren't arguing the point. We had expected to be there around 1:00 p.m., but our driving had been slowed down considerably due to poorer roads. Once we reached Multan, we spent over an hour trying to find our destination. The heat was unmerciful! We had traveled in temperatures up to 118 degrees. I had not eaten since the preceding noon, and was beginning to feel nauseous again, this time from hunger as well as from the heat.

Our reservations were at the Barrage Rest House, which was under the direction of the superintendent engineer of the Taunsa Project Circle. We drove around in circles, stopping frequently so that Aziz could ask directions to the Barrage Rest House. In despair, we watched as one after another of the natives shrugged his shoulders. The answers were always the same: "There are only three rest houses in Multan, and none of them are named Barrage." Finally we saw the sign. Clear as mud it read, "Canal (not Barrage) Rest House—Taunsa Project." It was now an hour later and we had found our destination, thanks to Aziz's perseverance, and the grace of God!

We spent two nights at the Canal Rest House, which was not as elaborate as the Sukker Rest House, but we found it to be very comfortable once we cooled down enough to enjoy it. Our accommodations included three bedrooms, two baths, a living room and a dining room. We had no idea where Aziz was sheltered, but he just disappeared every night when his work was finished, apparently to servant's quarters at each of our stops.

Early the next morning we set out with a guide to look over the City of Multan, an ancient city of 400,000 people enveloped with a thick curtain of birds and dust. Through it all, we were able to see impressive old brick buildings silhouetted against the sky. Of particular note was a beautiful old fort, situated high on a hill overlooking the City. We learned later that the ancient fort was Multan's prize bit of architecture.

Our guide took us into a building and down some steep winding stairs. This had originally been the entrance to a 300-mile tunnel that extended from Multan to Lahore but had since been blocked off and was used to display local products such as camel skin lamps, linens and pottery work.

From the fort, we drove close to the bazaars, parked, and set out on foot. The bazaars, which wound up and down the hill, looked like those in Karachi's old city but they seemed a bit cleaner—or were we just getting used to them? By the time we had gone half a block several hundred natives were following us. It wasn't until a man came up to Joyce and gingerly touched her platinum blonde hair that we realized she was the reason we were followed so often when we went out in public. We learned later that some of them thought that this little child with the platinum blond hair was a gift from Allah!

We hadn't traveled very far when we came upon a crowd of people surrounding a rickety flatbed truck upon which a troupe of transvestite dancers were performing. They had eyes that were heavily outlined in black soot, long black eyelashes, cheeks with heavy blotches of rouge circles, bright red lips, and gorgeous silk costumes. Wow! This was the first time I had seen transvestites, or had experienced one of their performances. As naïve as I was, it took me awhile to realize what we were witnessing.

By 10:00 a.m. it was so hot, we retreated to the rest house, determined to do any future shopping or sight seeing in late afternoon instead of in the morning. We shopped long enough to see wallas (merchants) with their fish, meat, candy and other foodstuffs lying out in the open, covered with flies. Not an ice cube in sight! There was no refrigeration. And as we made our way through the heat haze and back to the comfort of the rest house, I noticed sweat glistening on the copper shoulders of our guide, and felt drops of perspiration running down my face and back.

As we were eating breakfast the next day, a man we hadn't seen before kicked off his shoes, and walked towards our table with funny, mincing steps. He kicked his heels together and saluted Frank.

"Salaam, Sahib!"

"Salaam," Frank responded.

"I charge this rest house. Everything all right? Can show you some places in town? After you finish breakfast, Chief Engineer want meet you."

Frank assured him everything was satisfactory, so the visitor salaamed, clicked his heels again, and saluted. At the kitchen door, he put his shoes back on. Two seconds later, he was back again, shoes off.

"What time you go to town?" Same story, third verse, as he repeated those steps, this time asking, "How long you be in Multan?"

Shortly after we finished breakfast, Frank spent an enjoyable visit with the Chief Engineer who wanted to see him because he was "most eager that we had everything we desired." The little man with the mincing steps turned out to be our guide throughout the City of Multan, and a good one he was, too. Everywhere we went the people were so friendly and helpful that it made up for a lot of the inconveniences that we had encountered, such as a severe sandstorm that enveloped the city that afternoon.

The sandstorm was like a shroud in an eerie orange glow, reducing traffic to a crawl and sending hundreds with respiratory problems to hospitals. We had never experienced anything like it. We could hardly see our hands in front of our faces. The sandstorm caused the atmosphere to become dark as dusk at 2:00 p.m. when the sand began blowing and swirling furiously. The storm raged during the entire afternoon, remaining nearly as dark as midnight until after 5 p.m. The wind wrecked havoc everywhere. When it finally subsided, Multan was blanketed with thick layers of sand and dust that permeated everything that they touched.

We stayed two nights in Multan but found there was little to see but old forts, sand, dust, heat haze and buzzards. We had no misgivings about leaving that city early the next morning for Lahore.

CHAPTER TWENTY

LAHORE: "PARIS OF THE EAST"

Lahore, which is in the heart of the Punjab region, is known as the "Paris of the East" because of its climate, cultural centers, colleges and other attributes.

What a joy Lahore was! Compared to Karachi, it was an attractive city, quite modern, fairly clean, and so green it reminded me of Portland, Oregon. Donkey and camel carts were conspicuous by their absence on the Lahore streets; we saw modern buses, a modern traffic system (even one traffic light—the first one we'd seen since we arrived in the Middle East nearly a year ago), and visited their famous old Red Fort and many of their mosques, most of which were built during the reign of the first three great Mogul emperors. The third emperor, Shahjahan, is not only credited with building two of the most beautiful mosques in Lahore, but is credited with building the Taj Mahal in Agra, India. The tomb that he built in Lahore to honor his father, the second great ruler, Jahingir, is in my opinion almost as lovely as the Taj. The beautiful inlay work that decorated the interior of the mosque was almost identical to that of the Taj. Elaborate tiles in the glazed tile manner that was developed during the Moghul period adorned other tombs and mosques that were prevalent throughout the Punjab or Sind Provinces.

As we were photographing the famous Red Fort, the children excitedly pointed out dozens of sacred monkeys that were scampering around playfully on top of the fort's high walls, jumping over crevices and cavorting around.

We left Lahore about 10:30 a.m. three days later and headed for the India border 17 miles away. For the first time, I was grateful for being one of the "privileged few." Because we had Special Diplomatic Passports we were able to get through the five stops in an hour's time, whereas most of the natives had been squatting in the intense heat for hours, and sometimes days trying to get through customs. The customs officials were housed in a little straw hut, ignoring a mass of yellow jackets that were swarming around their heads as a teenaged boy squatted on the floor, swinging a large fan back and forth over their heads. They were in no hurry to rush through examining our documents. The only sign of speed in this hour was Aziz as he tore out of a hut with a swarm of yellow jackets behind him. When he bent down to pick up Frank's briefcase, he got some bees inside of his shirt and ended up with five bee stings.

CHAPTER TWENTY-ONE

NEW DELHI, AGRA AND THE TAJ MAHAL

Seeing Sikhs firsthand, now that we were on the Indian side of the border, was fascinating to all of us. They were the race of people that most of us at home associated with a "typical" Indian—long beard, and the long hair that is tied in a little bun above their foreheads. The Sikh religion forbids its followers to cut their hair during their lifetime, hair that is covered with wrapped turbans, often a beautifully tied turban of brilliant hues. We had heard so much about the viciousness of these people that we viewed them with mixed emotions—curiosity and apprehension. The Sikhs were the race that was blamed for much of bestiality that took place between India and Pakistan during Partition seven years earlier. However, we became acquainted with several Sikhs when we were in Delhi and to our surprise found them to be fun-loving and friendly.

The road to Delhi was better than those we experienced in Pakistan, and the countryside was pleasant and verdant. We saw cows and monkeys roaming freely in the fields. They are considered sacred, and severe penalties are applied if one should kill or hurt one of them.

"Look at that sign!" Judi exclaimed. The inscription on the sign read something like: for killing a cow, 50 rupees; a monkey, 25 rupees; and a woman, 10 rupees!

"There's a pig! Over there. Look!" Doug shouted, pointing at a wild pig that was foraging for food in a pile of rubbish. "That's the first pig I've seen all year!"

Monkeys roamed wild along the highways, and we chuckled at their antics. When we tried to take pictures of them, they would grab their young close to their chests and scamper off into the brush chattering excitedly as they scolded us for intruding on their privacy.

Immediately we sensed that the Indians were better off than the Pakistanis—in spite of the caste system. The lower classes, dregs of the society, were pitifully poor, existing from day to day as they struggled to survive, but the general attitude of the people was different. They appeared to be happier; there didn't seem to be the feeling of oppression that was so prevalent in Pakistan.

As we neared Delhi, Frank suddenly groaned.

"Oh, my gosh! Do you know what I forgot?"

"No. What?"

"Jack's instructions! Lordy, Lordy, Lordy!" That man had spent half a day—literally—drawing us pictures of where to go so as to miss the "Old City." Jack had also included the name of a hotel where we were to meet him so that he could personally lead us to his house, and Frank had left all of this information at home!

Naturally, we wound up in the Old City and within minutes were enveloped in a solid mass of bicycles, rickshaws, horse tongas, thieves and the lowest class of humanity for which the area was known. There was no turning back. We inched our way ahead with the tide as it were, and wondered if it would *ever* end. After we tangled with a rickshaw, and a horse tonga tangled with us, we were finally pushed clear of the Old City and made desperate attempts to find our friend's house. It was a sad bunch of Tessitors that straggled in to the Robison home two hours later.

We stayed in Delhi seven days, although 2½ of those days were spent in Agra viewing the Taj Mahal and other historic points. Ruth and Jack were perfectly marvelous hosts and did everything they could to show us a good time. They had a dinner party for us the night following our arrival, and a cocktail party of 80 or so people a few nights later. At their party, I wore a beautiful new blue silk dress, ballerina length. The matching shoes that I had ordered weren't finished on time, so I wore a new pair of wedges that were made by a shoe walla in Karachi. The toe came loose, so I put on a pair of new flats. The strap broke. We repaired the strap with nails from the first pair. We finally arrived at the party, which was held on Robison's breezy roof top, and my light silk dress flew over my head.

Thank goodness I had a respectable cotton dress waiting to be worn. It stayed down where it belonged!

Ruth chauffeured me around Delhi from morning to night, taking me from shop to shop as I frantically tried to complete my shopping. Prices were better in Delhi; the money exchange rate was higher, and the quality of most items was better. We rued the day that Frank was offered a job in Karachi instead of in New Delhi, which was loaded with points of interest and historical importance. In New Delhi, ancient mingled with modern in a pleasing mix. The city was more modern than Karachi or even Lahore, with a very nice shopping center. People were able to purchase almost anything they wanted "American style," or shop in the bazaars and go "native" if they wished. The climate was lovely while we were there, and we experienced none of the "beat" feeling from the weather as we had in Karachi.

The three-hour drive from Delhi to Agra was pleasant and scenic. As usual along the roads we saw the primitive conditions under which the indigents lived and worked. We saw many coolies, the most colorful native women we had seen to date, dressed in brilliant shades of deep yellows, oranges and bright reds. Many of them carried big straw baskets filled with gravel on their heads, swishing them back and forth like metronomes as they spilled gravel onto the roads. Coolies seemed to be everywhere, trudging to and from the wells with as many as three clay pots of water on their heads at one time. Agra itself was a typical native village. Dirty and primitive bazaars lined both sides of the main street, but the surrounding countryside was green. We attempted to take pictures of native life in the village, but doubted if they would turn out well because the natives followed us by the hundreds and crowded so close that we were prevented from shooting the pictures we wanted to take.

The beauty of the Taj was simply indescribable! We were afraid we would be disappointed; that it had been overrated, but not so! Our inability to properly describe the beauty of the Taj through the medium of words put us in a class of thousands before us who had had the same predicament. The day was cloudy when we first saw the Taj, and as we stood there, the sun came out and shone vibrantly on the white marble structure, giving it an ethereal aura. We had been advised to see the inside of the Taj during daylight; the outside of the Taj at night during a full moon. To our disappointment that night, even though the moon was full, it was too cloudy to see either the moon or the Taj.

To imagine that this building had been constructed in 1632—over 300 years earlier—and that all of the blocks of marble (and they were *huge)* were placed one on top of the other by primitive methods is hard to imagine.

Known as the "Glory of Agra," the Taj is situated on the right bank of the Jumna River. It was built by Shahjahan as a tomb for his favorite wife, Mumtaz Mahal, who died giving birth to their fourteenth child after 17 years of marriage. Historians and writers over the years have tried to find words to adequately depict its beauty, but all have failed. One writer seems to have come the closest when he described it as "the gorgeous romance of wedded love—the peerless white monument and the fairest shrine ever raised to love." Shahjahan's grief was intense. For weeks he refused to see any of his courtiers, or conduct affairs of state. Within two years, his hair had turned silver gray. He visited her grave every Friday, and became obsessed with building a tomb memorializing her that would surpass anything the world had ever seen, or would ever see.

Plans for the Taj were developed in 1631, the year after her death at age 39, and four years after Emperor Shahjahan's accession to the throne. Shahjahan invited eminent architects, masons and artists from his own territories and from foreign countries such as Persia, Arabia and Turkey to design and draw plans for the magnificent structure. Workers included laborers, designers, calligraphers, draftsmen, sculptors, mosaicists, inlayers and a dome-maker. Twenty thousand artists took 21 years to complete the exquisite masterpiece but to this day, the identity of the designer is unknown. The perfect symmetry of its exterior, the magnificence of its dome and minarets, the ornamentation and decoration, the beautiful floral design and charming mosaic work, and breathtaking style and beauty were (and are) beyond description.

The only part of the elegant edifice that lacked perfect symmetry were the tombs themselves. Shahjahan had started to build a monument to himself of black marble across the lake from his wife's when he died. His son Aurangzeb, who cared not for his father, and not for aesthetics, placed Shahjahan's tomb next to her tomb, throwing the symmetry off balance.

Their actual tombs were located in the basement of the Taj, and directly above them were replicas that could be viewed by the public. In the past, only the family could worship at the actual tombs, but at the time of our visit, they were open to the public as well. The tombs had been covered entirely with inlaid floral designs of precious and semi-precious stones—long since stolen. The entire interior of the Taj was inlaid with intricate carvings out of huge slabs of marble that took as long as 10 years each to carve. There was no piecing—all carving was done perfectly out of solid slabs of marble. We were deeply impressed by the inlaid mother-of-pearl designs that were on walls throughout the interior of the Taj. There was evidence that at one time precious and semi-precious stones, gifts from rulers of other countries or by nobles of his own kingdom, had been imbedded as well. Materials and gems came from all over the world. The white Makrana marble was brought from Jaipur, the red sandstone from Fatehpur Sikri, diamonds from Panna, turquoise from Tibet, lapis lazuli from Ceylon, jasper from Bombay, malachite from Russia, cornelian from Baghdad, chrysolite from the Nile and other precious stones and jewels from various other countries. This building was awesome. It truly deserves its place as one of the Seven Great Wonders of the World!

Shahjahan built most of the marble buildings inside Agra Fort as well as the Taj Mahal. After the first 11 years of Shahjahan's reign at Agra, in 1658, Aurangzeb usurped the throne and imprisoned his father in the Agra Fort. Shahjahan and his favorite daughter and constant companion were imprisoned in the fort until his death in 1666. Aurangzeb proclaimed himself emperor, put all of his brothers to death should there be any dispute over the throne, destroyed many famous Hindu temples at Benares, Muttra, and other places, and with their materials built several mosques. He also closed the schools to Hindus, burned and destroyed libraries and ancient books and revived a devastating poll tax on non-Mohammedans. He died at age 90 and was buried in an ordinary tomb. Served him right, we thought!

Forts, all complete walled cities, were evident in every city that we visited, but in my opinion, none of them came close to the famous Red Fort of Agra, where Shahjahan was imprisoned. Begun by Akbar in 1565 (a year after the birth of Shakespeare), it is a semi-circular palatial stronghold of decorative Moghul architecture as well as delicate inlay and beautiful relief in white marble. Despite the passage of so many years the citadel, designed and built by Akbar, and added to by Emperors Jahangir and Shahjahan, was still in a near-perfect state of preservation.

To the southeast of Jahangiri Mahal, was Akbari Mahal, which had been identified as the southern section of the Great Moghul's seraglio. Although in ruins, it was possible to discern the three sets of apartments where the ladies of the harem resided. Each apartment was named after the particular days of the week on which the Emperor visited, and a fifth set of women's apartments was there for foreign women who were brought there for the pleasure of the king.

The Red Fort measured one and a half miles in circumference, and was surrounded by a double wall of sandstone that was almost 70 feet high, pierced with four heavily fortified gateways. The Fort was enclosed within two paved moats; the outer one, 25 feet wide, and the inner one, 5 feet deep and 30 feet wide. The most significant building in the fort was Jahangiri Mahal, a two-story majestic edifice of red sandstone, intricately carved with birds, lotus and other designs.

We were impressed by our visit to Fatehpur Sikri, another walled city which was begun by Akbar (the first great ruler) in 1569 and completed in 1574, the year the Red Fort was completed. In Fatehpur Sikri we saw the famous Priest's Tomb, which was solidly encrusted with mother-of-pearl design of many different colors, and the separate buildings that Akbar built for his three favorite wives, plus the common courtyard for the rest of his harem. Ralph Finch, one of the first Englishmen to visit the area, wrote:

> *Agra is a very great city—with a fair castle with a large ditch. From there, we went to Fatehpur Sikri, which was the place where the King kept his court. The town is larger than Agra but the houses and streets are not as good. The king hath in Agra and Fatehpur Sikri, 1,000 elephants, 30,000 horses, 1,400 tame deer, 800 concubines and such store of leopards, tigers, buffaloes, cocks and hawks, that it is very strange to see.*

I hated to leave Agra. There was so much history there. I found myself wondering why the area wasn't better known as a tourist attraction. I hoped that we could return and spend a lot more time studying the ruins and artifacts, and learn more about the history of the region.

Hard as it was to leave Agra, it was equally hard to leave New Delhi and the surrounding area. It was time to come back to earth! There was much to see and we had barely touched the surface.

CHAPTER TWENTY-TWO

KYBER PASS: OMINOUS AND AWESOME

We bade goodbye to the Robisons and re-crossed the Indian/Pakistani border, again with a minimum of delay (Aziz stayed clear of the bees this time). I was so grateful that we were more fortunate than those poor wretched souls who had been squatting for endless hours in the broiling sun waiting for their turn to go through customs.

We stayed in Lahore that night, and the next morning drove to Abbotabad, our cook/bearer's village. Abbotabad is the place I liked the best—a quaint, primitive village, the hilliest, greenest place I had ever seen. Here we were to look up Sayeed Kahn and Ozmut Kahn, two of our friends who were Chief Aides-de-Camp to the Governor General, and were visiting there in an official capacity with the G.G. We were told they were at the Polo Grounds, so we drove down there in time to see them and two other G.G. bodyguards compete in a polo match on horseback. That's the sport to watch! Exciting!

The elite Governor General's Bodyguard Corp display magnificent horsemanship on their prize Arabian steeds. Not only were the Arabian steeds highly prized, but so were the Governor General Bodyguards. They not only were expert horsemen, but they were the crème de la crème of the Pakistani military, chosen for their integrity, loyalty, honesty, marksmanship and magnificent physical attributes. Without exception, they were all superb masculine specimens, ramrod straight, and over six feet in height.

After the match, Ozmut and Sayeed invited us to dinner at their club, and persuaded us to stay over an extra day at Ozmut's cousin's house to do some shooting and fishing up in the hills. Ozmut, driving a Jeep, led the way. Thank goodness, because for the next 45 minutes we bumped along dodging ruts and rocks on a road that was clearly meant for a Jeep, not a Chevrolet. We finally reached our destination, where before our eyes was a lovely ranch house situated alongside a sparkling brook. Overhead, branches from two huge trees provided welcome coolness and shade from the tropical heat. Behind the house, cascading down the mountains was a spectacular array of green trees, scenery for which we were all hungry.

We had a wonderful time with our friends and Ozmut's relatives. His cousin was a gorgeous Pakistani—shapely, 17 years of age, and ravishing in a lovely, red shalwar costume. The girl and Ozmut seemed to be very fond of each other, and I was surprised to learn that his parents had arranged his engagement, not to her, but to her older sister, when he was seven years old! What a pity they couldn't marry each other, I thought.

Taking my eyes off of Ozmut and his cousin, I turned to watch the others who were fly-fishing. What fun! The water was icy cold and so clear you wanted to drink it. Later, we watched in admiration as Ozmut and Sayeed, both sharpshooters, did some target practice.

We left Aziz with his family in Abbotabad, and set out for Peshawar with a Major from the Pakistani Cavalry who was also going to Peshawar. Peshawar is known as the garden spot of Pakistan, although to be honest, Major Shah showed us such a good time we saw very little of the city. He introduced us to the Commandant of the Kyber Rifles, the former Pier of Gilgat whom we had seen pictured in a recent *National Geographic* magazine. The Commandant invited us all to tea, and regaled us with stories about the rugged tribesmen, many of whom were "bad men not to be trusted." We were fascinated by his narration, and by the tribesmen who were scowling as they sauntered around town with rifles strapped over their shoulders.

He also described in detail the formidable mountainous area with its caves that wound endlessly for miles up to an altitude of 15,000 feet. He told us about an American couple, Jean and Frank Shaw, who had come to Pakistan to write a story on Gilgat, and how he had persuaded them to write a second story on all of Pakistan. When they completed the articles, the Commandant received notice that through the courtesy of the

Shaws he was being given a lifetime membership and subscription to the *National Geographic* magazine which pleased him no end.

What pleased us no end was his gift to us of a pair of straw shoes worn by the soldiers of the Kyber Pass area. The shoes were unique, with inch-thick noiseless straw soles, and straw flaps on top of the shoes that extended five inches beyond the toes.

"What are those things for?" Doug inquired, pointing to the flaps.

"When the guards are crawling around in the dark, searching for an enemy, or mines, and something touches the flaps, they rustle a little bit," the commandant replied. "The guards immediately suspect there might be danger and are prepared to react."

Joyce was intrigued by a ghurka knife, a big, curved blade about 14 inches long that was lying on a table nearby. The guard showed us three notches on the blade, and explained that whenever they cut off the head of an enemy, they would record the kill by cutting a notch in the blade. All three of the children grimaced. "What barbarians," Judi whispered, shivering.

When the time came to leave our new friends, the commandant supplied us with an armed guard for protection and gave us permission to bring our cameras along providing we took pictures only on the Afghan side of the border and photographed nothing of strategic importance on the Pakistani side. He bade us farewell and we headed for the Pass.

The Khyber Pass trip was as big a thrill for us, if not more so, than the Taj Mahal. You can hardly compare the two because the Taj had a majestic, regal type of beauty, whereas the Kyber Pass, with its austere, harsh, cold, ominous appearance gave us a thrill that was both awesome and frightening.

The Kyber Pass area was one of, if not *the*, most heavily guarded pass in the world at that time, if not at this writing in 2011. Our guard pointed out booby traps, mines, lookout posts and armed guards who seemed to be behind every rock and at the opening of every cave. Everybody was armed to the teeth, and we were grateful we had our big armed guard to protect us! The mountains were barren and rocky but the scenery was glorious. How we wished we could have taken pictures! The military officers at the Pakistan border served us tea and cookies and we visited with them as we watched Afghanis by the dozens walking across the border, toting belongings on their heads or backs, or leading donkeys that were laden with their worldly goods. As we watched, Judi playfully put her foot over the Pakistan/Afghanistan border. Immediately, armed guards jumped to attention, cocked their rifles and aimed them at her. She quickly stepped back, and the guards relaxed slightly. They had orders to shoot to kill if there was any question and nobody, not even a child, was exempt from suspicion. We learned in a hurry that they didn't play games with security, evidenced by the fact that nobody was permitted in the Kyber Pass area without permission.

Most of the area surrounding the N.W. Provinces were, or had been, tribal areas. The villagers had been fairly peaceful since Partition, but nobody was taking any chances. Every man we saw carried rifles over one or both shoulders. Nobody was allowed into some of the areas unless a truckload of 22 riflemen followed no further than 20 feet behind that person's car. We were no exception. Our neighbors had occasion to be grateful for that protection when their car frightened a camel that was carrying a child. The camel fell and landed on top of his saddle, but luckily the child jumped free, or there could have been an incident right there.

The second day we were in the N.W. Provinces, Major Shah took us up to the top of Kohat Pass, another tribal area where, again, every male inhabitant carried a rifle. We did not see a woman anywhere. The natives built their own little groups of huts, or villages, and every so often we passed a little group of mud huts that had been completely walled, and each one had its own lookout tower. In most cases, the huts were occupied by family groups and because intermarriage was the general rule, they stayed family groups.

We stopped at a little village whose inhabitants were famous for making rifles and guns entirely by hand using the most primitive of methods. We were amused to see that each one we picked was imprinted with words such as Winchester, Colt, Made in USA, Made in England, and names of manufacturing firms on the handles. They were afraid that the guns wouldn't work right if they didn't copy everything about the gun, or afraid that people wouldn't buy them if they knew that they had been made in Pakistan. Over Major Shah's objections, I bought a 38-caliber pistol.

"Jane, don't buy that one!" he cautioned. "It's made with inferior materials—from railroad ties—and will explode the first time someone shoots it!"

I bought it anyway, apologizing during the transaction because I had no intention of shooting the gun. Instead I wanted a souvenir that said "Made in Pakistan."

Mountain men, dressed in native garb of what appeared to be dirty homespun fabrics in muted earth tones, roamed the bazaar areas. The somber hues of the earth tones contrasted with the white (or what used to be white) tones of the cotton shalwar pants and long kamizs that were prevalent in the lowlands, was astonishing. Instead, the high altitude demanded warmer shalwar pants topped with long kamizs, vests and jackets. Sandals covered bare feet; and scarves which embraced necks, and turbans and/or caps that covered heads, were of wool. Part of the fashion statement was a rifle over one or both shoulders at the ready, accompanied by menacing scowls under heavy black beards. These mountain men were an element that indeed had to be reckoned with. I shuddered to think how easy it would be for a woman to be whisked away by these tribesmen, never to be seen again, and no one would be the wiser.

CHAPTER TWENTY-THREE

THE LAHORE FLOOD

The next day we picked up Aziz at his hut and met his wife and children again. His wife was plain and spoke no English, but was warm and friendly, as were his offspring. They were all dressed in colorful cotton shalwar outfits, and wore no jewelry. I liked them a lot. Their hut, although simple, was clean and comfortable. A lovely garden flourished outside the hut, and their cow was contentedly chewing her cud nearby. We chatted briefly with Aziz interpreting, and before long said farewell to Aziz's family and headed back to Lahore.

About six miles outside of Lahore, it started to rain. By nighttime, it was raining nearly as hard inside of our hotel room as it was outside. We were hopping up every few minutes, shoving the furniture around in vain attempts to locate some dry spots in the room. Our accommodations in Peshawar had been horrible. There, I swore the bathrooms had come over on the ark, but by the time we got out of Lahore, we were wishing we had the ark to put our bathroom in! The City of Lahore looked like a wild lake the next morning. It was raining furiously but we felt if we could only get out of Lahore all would be sunshine and bliss. Not so!

We fought our way inch by inch for over two hours trying to get out of the city limits. Innumerable times we were turned back by natives shouting at us and indicating the depth of the water ahead by pointing to their waists, their chests, or their shoulders. The water in places was from four to six feet deep. People were fleeing their huts by the hundreds, carrying their meager belongings in their arms or on their heads or backs. The rain was pouring so hard we could hardly see in front of us. We held our breath every inch of the way for fear the car would stop because we were driving in water two feet deep.

Two hours and numerous detours later found us about 10 miles out of Lahore, but it was too risky to continue. There were reports of a washed-out bridge ahead of us, and our brakes were so wet that if there had been a hill we never could have stopped. Some way, I don't know how, Frank managed to turn the car around and we tried to fight our way back to the city. To our dismay, we learned that the road back to Lahore had been blocked off. By coincidence, a man flagged our car and asked us if we would take him in to town. There was no more room in the car, but Aziz stood up to give him his seat, and it turned out to be a blessing. Our passenger was a road engineer and son-in-law of the Deputy Health Director of Lahore. He knew the streets well and directed us onto side streets until we reached his father-in-law's house. My heart sank when he asked Frank to drive up to the front door. Their yard was as big as a city block and the further in we drove, the deeper the water became. Finally we made it to the front door. We surveyed the situation with apprehension. The water was above the opening of the car door, so we sent the children out through the car's window. I thought about following suit but, surveying my hips, decided I didn't want to risk being stuck in the car window, so we opened the door quickly and I dashed out, as did the others. Frank quickly drove the car out to the street and waded back to the house in water that was above his knees.

Our passenger's father-in-law, Mr. Khan, was wonderful to us. He welcomed us, served us tea, and insisted we stay for lunch. I felt a little foolish at the table with no other women present. Women in Pakistan were not included at their husbands' tables unless given a special invitation, and must *under no circumstances* eat before the men did even if they are not eating with their husbands. While we were seated at the table, a succession of women were peeking out at me from the kitchen. I imagine they were not only curious but were probably horrified that I had the audacity to be there with the men!

By 1:00 p.m. the rain had let up somewhat and the water had receded a few inches, so we took our leave and fought our way back to the hotel. You can't imagine the misery and suffering that was everywhere. Several children had been drowned and wherever we looked we could see cars, trucks, and horse tongas stranded—some of them up to their rooftops in water. I think it was purely by the grace of God, and the fact that our Chevy turned amphibious, that our car was able to make it through. The rainstorm was unprecedented in Lahore history—it had rained 15.34 inches in 33 hours, most of it during the first 12 hours.

Devastation was everywhere. Natives by the hundreds were huddled under wet blankets, shivering with the wet and the cold with no place to go to dry off and get warm. Most of the little straw huts had either collapsed or had been completely inundated. The next day we tried to leave Lahore again only to be stopped by officers 27 miles outside of Lahore and be told that the road was still underneath four feet of water, and we had to take a 50-mile detour. On the detour, we went through one area that was two miles long with water at least two feet deep. There were no trees to mark the side of the road, but the natives had had the foresight to pull up bushes and mark the edge of the road with their branches. It was only after we observed a bus getting through that we dared to try it. It was a strange feeling—to drive in a lake.

We spent that night in Multan, and it wasn't until the next morning that I realized the boxes inside of our car were soaked. I spent an hour unpacking the "treasures" I had purchased in India, much to Frank's annoyance because he had wanted to get an early start. All of the shoes we bought were soaking wet, so was my lovely new evening bag (not, of course, the cheap straw one.) I was devastated to discover that all of the beaded evening bags and belts that I had purchased for a friend in Karachi were soaked. I didn't expect her to even want them, but when we got home I dried them in the sun and went over them with a steam iron and they seemed none the worse for wear. Luckily, the water didn't tarnish the beadwork, and she was thrilled with the purchases. The only item that had escaped the ravages of the water was a box of silk material.

We finally started out at 4:00 a.m., bypassed Sukker, and drove straight through to Karachi. We reached home at 10:30 p.m. with Joyce running a high fever. We learned later that she and I had both picked up bacillary dysentery somewhere along the way and we suffered with it for several days.

We had been so anxious to get home, but upon our return, one look at the house and we wondered why! Our hamal, Ali Gore, who had little to do but keep the dogs fed and dry, was asleep in one of our beds upstairs; the house was dirty; our dachshund, Mem Sahib, and her pups were boarded up in the "swimming pool" instead of in the room that I had specified, and were shivering on sopping wet blankets in their beds;

there was evidence that card parties had been held in the house; and one of the servants across the street had been running a house of prostitution in our servants' quarters! We were furious, and Aziz lost face; he had had so much faith in the man. Needless to say, Ali Gore was fired on the spot. Once again, we found ourselves trying to find a good hamal, but our quest proved to be a difficult, if not an impossible task.

The turnover of hamals at our house during the past year was incredible. First, Abdullah was with us for six months. His work was mediocre, but he was the one who stank. It became so bad that his body odor permeated the rooms long after he had worked in them, so we had to let him go. We then hired the cutest little 14-year-old boy who was more decorative than he was capable; next we hired a fellow who worked across the street, but he changed his mind and remained where he was with a new family. (They fired him a few days later after learning he was the man who ran the brothel in our servant's quarters.) As a replacement, he sent his cousin to work for us, but the cousin turned out to be dishonest. Aziz told me later that he had been fired from his previous job for "having peoples, not his wife, in his quarters." Enter Ali Gore. We had to pay a large vet bill because our dachshund developed rheumatism, strep throat and the flu from living on wet blankets in the room that seeped water. Ali Gore was out. Our sweeper then agreed to be sweeper/hamal, but his wife was on her deathbed so for three weeks we didn't have a sweeper or a hamal. When he returned after his wife died, he realized that the two jobs were too much to handle, so he stayed on as sweeper and Goldfranz became our new hamal. Goldfranz sat more than he stood the first day, and the second day, announced that he had worked so hard the day before that he had gotten a fever and couldn't work anymore. Ghulam was hired next. His work was fine, but 12 pounds of butter and 12 pounds of sugar disappeared within two weeks after he began working for us. Doug decided to take care of the problem himself one day by telling Ghulam the sugar was wrapped in "pig grease".

"No," Ghulam said.

"Sure, it says so right here. Read it!" Doug said pointing at the printing on the package and knowing full well that Ghulam didn't know how to read. When we realized how much he was shorting us on food that he purchased in the market, we let him go and hired Nazir. Nazir had a pleasant disposition, and seemed to be a good worker—said he knew every job and would do any job. His second day, he refused to do the floors among other things, and still expected 80 rupees a month pay. Exit Nazir; enter Hascham. Hascham learned I wasn't too happy with his work, so after nine days he quit. We then hired Aziz's cousin Gonney as hamal. After Gonney's third day, Aziz came to me and said Gonney was gone. Foolishly I had given him a day off the same day that Aziz had a day off, and he promptly got a job for more money. He stayed on his new job one day, then came back to us. I liked him fine, and hoped he would stay with us. Needless to say, at this point, we were sick and tired of hamal problems!

By this time, Aziz was tired of hauling water from next door. Ever since the monsoon, our water had been contaminated with a saturated solution of salt water, flavored with refuse from an overflowing septic tank.

Finally, three weeks later, AID sent someone over to build a new water tank. The tank collapsed. Seems the repairman used 8 parts sand to 1 part cement. That was more than Aziz could bear. He quit!

Aziz returned in a day or two, apologized and was back in the fold, much to our relief. I was amused when word got back to me that the neighbor's cook had said, "I knew Aziz come back. He and Mem Sahib [meaning me] right for each other!"

When Aziz quit it was the last straw! We could see the only answer was to get a different house, and to get it in a hurry. We felt that we had served our time in the Crazy House. Officials at the Embassy said we could have another house, that we were next on the list, but that none were available at the moment. So once again, we waited.

We had been home from our trip only a few days when Aziz came to us on the verge of tears, wailing "My boy gone! He took off. No know where he gone! He took rupees—100 rupees, luggage, clothes. He say nothing. He gone!"

Aziz's son was 17, and had always seemed like such a nice young man. He must have been in some kind of trouble, because while we were on our trip he spent a lot more money than he should have, borrowed from a couple of people and sold some of Aziz's silk. Frank and Aziz left immediately to see if they could find him at the railroad station. They succeeded, and it became Aziz's job to deal with his son.

Me? I was going to lose my mind, but before doing so, I planned a trip to Bombay with Josie Armstrong, my French friend.

CHAPTER TWENTY-FOUR

BOMBAY, A SHOPPER'S PARADISE

Josie and I left our husbands, my kids, our servants, and all worries behind, and hopped a plane to Bombay. Never mind that it took five hours flying time as opposed to two hours for most of the other planes. We enjoyed the flight and felt free as birds. The flight was relaxing and fun, and upon landing we were met at the airport by a driver in the hotel limousine.

We had reservations at the beautiful Taj Hotel with a lovely room that overlooked the bay. The room was decorated American style with attractive furniture and carpeting, Venetian blinds (the only ones we had seen in the Middle East), and lovely décor. White ceramic tiles covered the walls and the floor in the bathroom, and there was *hot water!* We indulged ourselves luxuriously in hot baths after all of our frantic shopping sprees. All of this for 55 rupees ($12) a day! Pure luxury! The hot baths alone were worth the trip to Bombay, we decided.

We found Bombay to be a seaport town bustling with activity. It appeared to be more metropolitan than New Delhi, with fewer Sikhs, just as many beggars, and as many persistent shopkeepers standing outside of their shops trying to lure us inside.

Bombay was known as a shopper's paradise. But one night we thought we wouldn't live to tell the tale.

That night we were startled when the phone rang at 10:00 p.m. It was a jeweler wanting to know if we were going to come to his shop to see some stones or not, as we promised we would do. We didn't want to go out that late at night, but agreed, albeit reluctantly. He met us at our hotel within minutes and led us out into the murky, starless night. We followed him by foot down the narrow, unlit street, stumbling along, groping our way. It was pitch dark, and eerily quiet. The only lights were from some fires and lamps in front of huts or shops; the only noise was that of an occasional baby crying or a dog barking. We had walked now for 20 or so minutes. The further we went, the more anxious we became. We had no idea where we were, and didn't know if we could trust this stranger or not.

"What are we getting into?" Josie wondered, shivering. "We don't even know this man. Where is this stranger leading us?"

Just then the jeweler turned into a run-down alley that was filled with pot holes and a benjo ditch (an open ditch filled with human waste.) It seemed to be even darker than the other street had been. Pye dogs howled in the distance. Another baby cried, and kept on crying.

"This is eerie," I whispered. Despite the fact that a close friend had recommended the jeweler, we continued to be suspicious of him.

Eventually, he turned into another alley. After a short distance, he guided us up some rickety stairs and led us down a long, dark hallway with squeaky planks. I jumped as a rat squealed and skittered against my ankles before disappearing out of sight. Josie and I both wanted to run, but to where?

We were terrified as the jeweler turned the key in a lock and bade us enter. He locked the door from the inside and turned on the light. We didn't know if we should run or scream. It was only after he turned on another light and removed two trays of stones from a safe that we were able to relax. His stones turned out to be beautiful, but we were aghast at the way he was doing business.

After examining his stones, I bought a gorgeous cornflower blue star sapphire for $500 (much less than a similar stone would have cost in the States), and Josie coveted a lovely ruby, but didn't buy it. I was thrilled with my purchase, despite the unorthodox way the jeweler did business. Josie fussed all of the way to Karachi because she hadn't bought the ruby.

Because we could carry more purchases on board ship, we elected to return to Karachi by boat instead of by air. The boat ride was serene and delightful, except for Josie's fussing. We were rested and more than willing to tackle the problems at home. All in all, our shopping trip to Bombay was successful, and an adventure that for the most part we enjoyed!

CHAPTER TWENTY-FIVE

PAKISTAN'S YOUNGEST CHIEF MINISTER

As Frank's responsibilities increased so did his travels to, among other destinations, East Pakistan, Lahore, Afghanistan, Japan and occasionally to Iran. Along with his added responsibilities, we gained many pleasant friendships.

Among our new friends was Ali Martabat Mukhdumzada Syed Hassan Mahmud, Chief Minister of Bahawalpur State. Mahmud, a 31-year-old widower, was handsome and suave. An egotist to be sure, but one of the most charming and interesting people we had met in Pakistan. Our friendship began when Frank was made project advisor of the additional projects, one of which had to do with the water problems in Bahawalpur State. Thus it was that one day we received an impressive formal invitation encrusted with Mahmud's official seal, inviting us to a "small" (20 couples) dinner party at his executive mansion.

On the appointed day, we drove to his mansion, parked on the street and walked into the compound, up the circular drive surrounded by a beautifully manicured lawn that was framed by a profusion of tropical blossoms, dodging chauffeured limousines as they glided past us, depositing notables such as His Excellency Mamdot the Governor of Sind Province at the front entrance. The impressive guest list also included Pakistan's Minister of Defense, two young and very handsome colonels and their wives, several American couples and finally, Mr. Nazam, a wealthy playboy from Bahawalpur Province, who drove himself there in his Buick convertible with his pet leopard regally occupying the passenger seat beside him. Nazam jumped out of his convertible and proceeded to lead his leopard to the front door. Mahmud, a virtual dictator, albeit a charming one, let it be known in no uncertain terms that he was *not* in favor of the leopard and ordered Mr. Nazam to return the leopard to his car "immediately!" Mahmud later confided in us that he had told his playboy friend that he would appoint him a Minister if he got rid of his leopard, and if he got married and settled down. "He likes to play too much," Mahmud said, exasperated.

As we prepared to enter the two-story executive mansion, I noticed the exterior was stucco, and although the building was huge, it was nondescript in appearance. We were astonished to be personally ushered into the foyer by Mahmud himself. Two uniformed servants were standing at attention as Mahmud led us into an immense living room, then into the ballroom and eventually into the dining room. Huge crystal chandeliers were suspended from the high ceilings on what appeared to be the thinnest of crystal threads, and the floors were carpeted throughout with luxurious Persian carpets of superb quality. Objets d'art, collected from throughout the world, blended into the extravagant décor as if they had always belonged. The furniture was of teak, dark and massive, with intricate carvings and mother-of-pearl inlay work exemplifying the skilled workmanship of native artisans. The cushions and couches were upholstered in ornate brocades and exquisite brocade draperies which extended from the 20 foot ceilings to the marble floors. To say we were impressed, was an understatement. We were blown away!

Mahmud, self-assured, dynamic and exuding confidence in himself, was plainly revered by those who knew him. When he spoke, every person in the room fell silent, listening spell-bound to his words. I regretted the intrusion when the head bearer announced that dinner was served. Mahmud graciously took me by the arm and seated me on his right.

"Do you like to hunt, Mrs. Tessitor?" he began.

"I don't know anything about it," I admitted sheepishly.

"That is a pity," he said with his clipped British accent. "There is marvelous wild boar hunting in Bahawalpur Province. I'd like to invite you both to join us."

"We'd love to try," I answered quickly, doubting if Frank would like any part of that idea.

"Do you like to ride?" he continued. I groaned inwardly, saying I didn't know much about that either. (Even though I was taking riding lessons,

I was recalling the painful experience I had had years before when Frank had to bandage my backside for two weeks after I had been riding.)

When Mahmud asked "Do you like to fly?" I quickly answered yes, even though flying in small planes made me airsick.

"Marvelous, I've got my own plane. We'll go flying some day." By that time I felt like an absolute dud! He promised to arrange a trip to his state in the fall, and include all of these sports in the itinerary, plus elephant rides, fishing, and "anything else you want to do."

The banquet, beautifully served by waiters in crisp, starched uniforms and turbans with high, plaited plumes, was extraordinary—an endless variety of curries scented with cardamom, curry powder, saffron, turmeric, cumin seed, cloves, coriander, fenugreek, black pepper, cayenne pepper and other exotic spices of the Middle East. The dinner also featured kebabs on skewers, meat balls, lamb, mountains of rice with raisins, chappatis (unleavened bread), quail, fricassee chicken, vegetables and coconut. Dessert consisted of pineapple ice cream and mangoes. I had not tasted mangoes before. Mahmud insisted that I try some, preparing them for my plate himself. What a pleasant surprise. They were wonderful! The cuisine was divine, the conversation stimulating, the ambiance, out of this world.

During the dinner I asked Nazam if my children could see his leopard. He was glad to oblige and we arranged to meet at the Crazy House for tea. Never in my wildest dreams did I ever think I would be entertaining a leopard in my living room, but that's exactly what I did the next afternoon at 4 p.m. After I took a picture of Nazam, the leopard, and Doug in the yard, we proceeded into the living room. Before sitting down, Nazam had his servant remove my coffee table from a Bokara rug, the only rug we owned, so that his 14-month-old pet could lie down on it and "be more comfortable" than he would be if he were lying on the cold terrazzo floor. The servant then put a pillow under the leopard's head and proceeded to wipe him down with a cloth the entire time Nazam and I enjoyed our tea. Before the afternoon ended, Nazam announced that he was "searching for a pair of lions" for his next pets. I surmised that it would be some time before Mahmud would bestow a Minister's title on him at the rate he was collecting wild animals for pets.

The banquet at Mahmud's was almost an out-of-this-world experience. He was an excellent host, and a sparkling conversationalist. Although he talked about himself a lot (a quality I usually found distasteful), our interest and our questions undoubtedly spurred him on. His well-developed ego and dynamic personality coupled with his extraordinary success as a politician electrified everybody in his presence.

"I am a direct descendant of Mohammad, the Muslim prophet," Mahmud said. "My father, who is a zamindar [large land owner], owns Bahawalpur Province. I'd like to take you and Mr. Tessitor there and show you manuscripts that we have, written in pure gold, that are several hundred years old, and one sword that is 1,100 years old. Our home and 18,000 acres of land in Bahawalpur Province comprise a complete city, enclosed within a stockade wall. There is no stealing within our city," he said proudly. "At night the gates are closed and no one is allowed to enter. It's all very safe and very private."

Lore has it that the village is beautiful beyond description and reverence towards Mahmud is such that the natives prostrate themselves in front of him and attempt to kiss his feet whenever he goes there.

Mahmud said when he was in school, his father gave him an allowance of 4,000 rupees ($1,000) per month, but then they had a falling out and he left home with 7 rupees in his pocket.

"How did you survive?" I asked.

"I went into the cotton ginning business. My family name was my collateral. Seven months later, I grossed 11 laks [$1,100,000].

"Amazing! When did you go into politics?"

"When I was 26. Five years ago. I became the youngest Chief Minister in the country. Since then, I was deposed during a military coup." He was reflective a moment, then grinned, "I'll come back. It's only a matter of time." He made the statement with finality, not conjecture.

We were intrigued with his comments regarding his childhood and his experiences, and I couldn't help but compare his pompous circumstances with those of the average, destitute Pakistani.

Mahmud seemed to have had a phobia about being alone, and constantly surrounded himself with others. Sometimes he would send his driver to our house early on Sunday mornings, often with a basket of mangoes or papayas, accompanied by a note: "Please come to bridge this morning at 9:00." The invitations were commands that we willingly obeyed, and within minutes we would be racing along to his mansion in his sleek, black Mercedes-Benz, comparing this luxurious feeling with mixed emotions as we dodged camel carts, donkeys and sweeper women. Upon our arrival, Mahmud would invariably assign Frank to be the Governor of Sind's partner, and would assign me to be his partner. Luckily, we had incredibly good luck together over the bridge table because the stakes were 1/20th of a point, which scared me to death as I thought my bridge rated only match-betting proportions.

Although the trip to Bahawalpur State did not materialize, we had many memorable parties, bridge games, and other social activities with Mahmud and his friends. One night he invited 21 of us "girls" to his mansion for dinner and took us all to the theatre afterwards. He drove five of us to the theatre in his deluxe convertible and I found myself wondering if that was what it felt like to be in a harem. As an aside, I was amused to discover that he always asked to see the guest list before he accepted an invitation to one of our parties. Upon reflection, I have often wondered if it was a form of snobbishness, or if he was concerned about his own safety.

Later, as we learned to know him better, I dared to ask him more pertinent questions, particularly about the political situation. His answers were guarded and shrewd and we realized that there was more about the intricacies of Pakistani politics than we would ever be privileged to learn. Nevertheless, the conversations we had with him were stimulating and more interesting than we had during our entire stay.

I had been looking for antique guns for a Denver friend, and Mahmud gave us a handsome old gun, said to be 400 years old, with a curved handle and gold and silver inlay design. He also gave us a gorgeous antique Bokara rug that was 6'x 9' with stitches that were unbelievably fine. They are both treasures.

One evening at a particularly lively discussion I asked Mahmud, "Are you in favor of democracy?"

"Yes," he responded without hesitation. "I'm in favor of democracy, but in Pakistan [Paw kis tawn] only a 'controlled democracy'. Our people are too illiterate. They are not ready yet for democracy as your country knows it."

CHAPTER TWENTY-SIX

FRANK EXTENDS HIS ASSIGNMENT

Before we traveled to India, Frank had made arrangements to extend our tour six months until May 1956.

Later, he agreed to return for another two years—until 1958. We then decided that following home leave, the children and I would stay in the States, and Frank would return to Pakistan for another two years by himself.

We had been concerned (needlessly it turned out) about the children's schooling, and also their health. Joyce had finally had her tonsils removed and was a lot healthier and happier; Judi had had surgery to remove a ganglia from her wrist that appeared to have been caused by her baton twirling, so she was more comfortable; and Doug was happier because more American boys had moved to Karachi and he had more playmates.

After we had returned from India, there had been a lot of farewell dinners for Americans who had completed their tours and were returning home, and a lot of "hello" and "welcome" functions for newcomers who were arriving to replace them. The period between September and December marked the end of a two-year stay for the original FOA (Foreign Operations Administration) personnel, so there was a big changeover.

We had settled in nicely and were prepared to stay another six months. I busied myself with bridge and painting lessons, the recreational program, and horseback riding lessons. To my delight, Sayeed and Ozmut continued to let Josie and me ride the G.G.'s horses. We had a lot of fun trotting and racing on the sandy beach that bordered the Arabian Sea, galloping along on packed sand with cool breezes blowing through our hair, without a care in the world. It was pure heaven!

Next to riding, my favorite pastime was painting. My instructor, Sheik Ahmed, painted a portrait of me. It was not a good likeness, but he wanted to add it to his collection. I, on the other hand, painted a portrait of Aziz, and another one of a Pakistani woman named Lily. The one of Aziz was a good likeness, but the painting of the woman was disappointing. I started out to depict a lovely Pakistani woman with a very unusual hairline. My instructor grabbed my brush and repainted the hairline so that it was no longer Lily! The portrait looked like any other native. It completely destroyed the portrait in my opinion! Except for that incident, I enjoyed painting a lot. For the first time in my life, I could lose myself completely in the process. I was grateful to have had the time and opportunity to paint—something I had never done before or since. It was a lot of fun, not only to paint, but to be associated with artists and art students. At one point, our friend, Ishmaili, painted a portrait of Doug with a palette knife and gave it to us for a Christmas present. It was an incredible likeness, one of the gifts I cherish the most.

The social scene after the holidays had slowed to a crawl, with the Valentine dance for Americans being the big exception. Frank and I won the door prize, a dance with Mr. and Mrs. Ambassador. The Ambassador didn't know how to dance, but we walked around the floor for four dances. He was feeling no pain, and was a terrific sport. No wonder. We found out later that they were mixing the martinis nine to one! Frank thoroughly enjoyed his dances with Mrs. Ambassador, saying, "That's the first time I ever won a prize that I couldn't take home with me."

Doug was the personality kid—a really good egg, and enthusiastic about activities such as his Boy Scout troop, but something was missing. He had few boys to pal around with, and he was becoming too used to being waited on by servants. For example, one day I was determined to teach him some manners, so as we pulled up in the car I asked him to please get out and open the car door for me. He grumbled and sputtered "women!" and reached for the door but the chowkidar beat him to it. I told Doug to let it go, he could open the front door for me instead. So, as he reached for it, the bearer quickly opened it from the inside! Another time, I asked Doug to pick up his clothes. "Why should I when they are being paid to do it?" was his retort.

Clearly, strict discipline at a private school would be good for him. Besides, we all agreed he needed to get away from his sisters for awhile. He decided he would like to join some of the other American children and go to school abroad. His first choice was a school in Switzerland, but he changed his mind in favor of the American School in Beruit, Lebanon. Between receiving a letter from the Beruit school saying they had room for Doug, and the nine days it took for our letter with the down payment to reach them, the school had been filled and he was placed on the waiting list. Beruit was said to be the "Paris of the East, the nicest place this side of Honolulu," and the American School was reputed to be one of the finest schools in the world. Because many of the children from Aramco Oil Company in Saudi Arabia went there, it filled rapidly. After the initial disappointment, we were glad it fell through because there were now 21 students in Doug's class. The American school in Karachi had become big business with 182 children enrolled, compared to the 33 that were enrolled when our children started.

Judi and about 12 other ninth graders became charter members of a high school correspondence course that was being formed for the first time at the UCLA Extension School. It was a tough course. All work had to be mailed to UCLA for grading, and although Judi had been a straight A student for the past two years at the Calvert School and was a conscientious worker, we were apprehensive about how well she could do under the new setup. She was taking difficult subjects—Latin, typing, algebra, English and history—but managed to do well in spite of the UCLA curriculum.

Joyce was still a platinum blond and was quite grown up in her actions, but like Doug, was becoming spoiled with all of the servants catering to her every whim. If I gave an order, and she gave another one, they did as she bid. I had to jump all over the mali for taking orders from her. You would think they all had rings in their noses, the way they jumped at her bidding!

Our life at the Crazy House had become almost unbearable. Our water tank had not been repaired since the monsoon. We were bailing three buckets of water a week out of the room that leaked water. For two months all we got out of our water pipes was a saturated solution of salt water, we still had to haul our drinking water and cooking water from next door, and when we took a bath we felt stiff when we emerged. I never did understand the details but it seemed as though the water came into our underground tank sans salt, but the tank was rotten so the same water that leaked into our basement room leaked into the water tank. We reached the point that we couldn't even open our eyes when we washed our faces because of the salt water. It was then, when the Embassy finally sent some men out to build us another water tank that Frank, in checking their work, dug his fingernail into the cement and the whole thing started to crumble. It turned out the water tank was being built with seven parts of sand to one part of cement. That was the last straw! We couldn't stand it another minute, and asked for another house. In due time, we were promised one that was under construction with a finish date expected to be December 20.

The new house was more like typical American houses. It was three blocks from the new American school, and two miles from the Crazy House. Since petrol was $1.09 an imperial gallon, the close proximity of the school was an important factor.

We moved into our new house at the end of February 1955—two months later than promised. On February 23, a couple of days after we moved in, I went to the Seventh-Day Adventist Hospital to have my head examined. No kidding! I had been pushing Joyce in her swing set, and the whole thing collapsed. The big three-inch iron pipe that went across the top came down on the top of my head and before I got out of the hospital, I had a hair cut, nine stitches and five shots. I was relieved that Joyce escaped without any ill effects. One of the swing set's stands fell across her shoulder, missed her head by a fraction of an inch, and as I lunged to grab it away from her, the rest of the set came down on top of me. The two-and one-half inch-long cut and resultant shots made me feel like a pin cushion. The swing set had collapsed because the movers had just stuck it on the yard without properly anchoring it.

A week later, I had the stitches removed and four days after that I was back in the hospital, this time with acute bronchitis. My temperature was 105 degrees when I entered, but it didn't take the hospital staff long to bring it down to normal. Their procedure was to wrap me in hot wet packs several times a day, take me, packs and all, to the basement where they threw buckets of ice water on me. No one had ever been as anxious as I was to leave that torture chamber after eight days of electro-and hydro-therapy treatments every day even if it meant going back to household problems. The only way I could go home was to promise the doctor faithfully that I wouldn't do a thing but rest for another week. Rest was welcome because after I hit my head, I had double vision and trouble focusing. X-rays determined that the problems were not serious but caused from pressure on the brain as a result of swelling.

While I was recuperating, I had a lot of time to compare life in the States with life in Karachi. Our friendship with Mahmud and others provided an insight into the wide disparity between the wealthy and the poor; there was a terrific gap in between. I wouldn't trade life at home for the pomp and ceremony that were so popular at the Governor General's monthly teas, or in State festivities, yet the appeal was hard to explain.

Whenever there were visiting dignitaries, the Pakistanis would block off the main roads for hours if the party were to travel along those roads. Police patrolled every half a block of both sides of the streets for miles and *nobody* dared to break through those lines. There was always a police escort preceding the official party—20 or 30 motorcycles; or sometimes the cavalry trotted ahead with cavalrymen wearing brilliant uniforms atop dashing Arabian steeds. Following the motorcycles or cavalry, was a division of Jeeps loaded with more uniformed servicemen, followed by officials of the highest order.

To see and hear the bagpipe bands, hear the fanfare as the G.G. and his official party descended down the steps onto the splendor of Persian carpets; to watch as he and his entourage were seated under the bright Shamivars [tents] strung overhead to ward off the sun; to see important dignitaries in their official uniforms, and to see and hear firsthand the G.G. making speeches that because of his stroke nobody could understand, made me wonder why they resorted to such ceremony. I couldn't decide in my own mind to be impressed or amused by such a show. I was glad we had occasion to join in, because most FOA people did not have that privilege. It was only because of our friendship with the G.G.'s bodyguards, Sayeed and Ozmut, that we were on the official list.

During my hospital confinement I was unable to attend an elaborate celebration in honor of King Hussain of Jordan, so Judi was selected to go in my place. The king was 16 years old at the time, and Judi was thrilled to talk to the Boy King (as he was known), obtain his autograph, and see the glamorous festivities.

We would have been hard pressed to attend similar State or social events in the States. From that and other points, living in Karachi had its advantages. But there was the other side. Unless they experienced the inconveniences that we endured, people at home could not have fully understood my complaints regarding having to do my own work—the cooking, shopping, dish washing as well as most of the house cleaning.

To elaborate, the cooking wasn't too difficult, except the kitchens were like saunas. I chose the hottest weather of the season to decide to go it alone. The weather for the most part was consistently over 110 degrees. The day the dhobi didn't show up for the third time in a row I decided to do ten days' wash. I was hanging clothes out on the line at 2:00 p.m. and learned the next day that the temperature was 114 degrees in the shade that afternoon. It's no wonder I was as wet as the wash.

During the cooking sessions my clothes got soaking wet from the skin out. One night Frank was beating some frosting for me and showed me his arm. The perspiration was running off as though he were under a shower. Our sink, like all Pakistani sinks, reached to my knees in the poorly-lit, window-less pantry between the cook house and the dining room. Every time we entered that tiny room it felt as though we were in a Turkish bath. As I've said, all drinking water had to be boiled, and all dishwashing water had to be heated on the stove. I put my back out, with no osteopath or chiropractor to put it back in place, lugging those big pans of water from the faucet (which was close to the floor in the cookhouse), over to the stove, and from there to the sink umpteen times a day. The kerosene stove cooked things nicely, although frequently when we thought something should be about done we discovered the stove had run out of kerosene—***again***.

Then there was the shopping. I reached the point where I didn't mind doing that too much, although every time I went to the market I would return home with a headache. We had to fight the urchins off—they wanted bachsheas (tips), and all wanted to be our coolies, or wanted to guard our car—for a price, of course. They would run half a block toward our car when they would see us parking, and fight amongst themselves in the hopes of getting the "job". I hired a 'regular' coolie at the bazaar when I could find him. He spoke a little English and helped me find some items that I needed. I also found a butcher who was fairly reliable. I learned to breathe to some extent in the meat market, and not make too many faces in the fish market. I learned how to carry home live crab, and dead beef, all loose in the same basket with tomatoes and potatoes. I learned to jump across the sewage streams that filtered in and around the market, and learned to park on the opposite side of the benjo ditch. I even got used to seeing men going to the bathroom. (They usually turned to a fence or a rock as they squatted, but not always, and it didn't seem to bother them if someone saw them in action).

Then, there was the dust. I knew finally, why they favored the type of brooms that they used. The branches with their feathery leaves were ideal to sweep up the fine sand and dust, although I still hadn't learned how to scoot on my haunches like the natives did when I was sweeping.

Our brooms didn't begin to pick up the dust and sand.

Theirs did.

During the time I was without a cook or hamal, our gardener was the saving grace. I could not have managed without his help! I had fired our cook/bearer five weeks earlier, on May 20 to be exact. It broke my heart, but his foul disposition was getting too much to bear. I fired him when he had another of his snits, and swore I would *never* take him back.

Frank and I had invited 21 guests to our house for dinner the night Aziz left in a huff. Not only did he quit on the spot, but he took his cousin Gonney, our hamal, with him. It was 10:30 a.m., 112 degrees in the shade, the breakfast dishes had not been washed, the beds weren't made, and nothing had been started for dinner. As you can imagine, I cooked like mad all day. During the dinner we managed fine, though, with help from God and two bearers that I had hired to help serve.

Aziz owed us 290 rupees when he left, which was nearly $100. The next day I received a letter from him telling us we owed him 375 rupees, 8 annas for the preceding month, which we had already paid. He also ignored the fact that of the amount he claimed we "owed him" he had already borrowed 50 rupees.

I was terrified. I knew he was desperate for money, and feared he might try to kidnap Joyce to get it. Instead, he went back to his village and had the village "secretary" write us a letter apologizing, saying his brain hadn't been working. We thought he was temporarily out of his mind because he was nearing the end of Ramazan. The heat was unmerciful, causing many people to become addled. He asked us to give him his job back, but we ignored the letter. On June 20, he returned to Karachi with his wife #2 and their 14 month old child, having sent wife #1 and his other children by her back to his village with our hamal when he left in May. Once again Aziz asked for his job back. I was resolute. No way!

About this time, we hired Mohammed, a highly recommended bearer. It was my intention to do the cooking. Can you believe, three days later I hired Aziz back? Only this time, we hired him back as cook only, with a 10 rupee cut in pay.

Everyone, me included, thought the heat had gotten to my brain, too, when I took him back. But, in spite of everything, I liked him. He had a lot of good points, and I had spent a lot of time training him. We told him the setup, and said if he could get along with our new bearer, we would give it a try. It worked beautifully—***for five days!*** Since then, I've tried as many cooks as we did hamals a year ago. Only this was worse. Aziz blackballed us at the market so it was virtually impossible to attract a first class cook. He ran us down so terribly that good cooks didn't come by for an interview; those that weren't desirable flocked to the house in droves. The last anyone saw of Aziz he was running down the road screaming at the top of his lungs.

I tried six or seven cooks, and believe me, they were the bottom of the barrel. I finally found one that was fairly good, mediocre, actually, but he stole too much from us. In one week's shopping, Ghulam charged us for 19 1/2 lbs. of meat and two chickens, despite the fact that we were small eaters. After I fired him, I agreed to try him a little longer when he promised to be more careful with his purchases. He then bought 16 lbs. of meat and one chicken in three weeks to illustrate how much he had been over-charging us to begin with. Soon after Ghulam arrived, Mohammed left to bring his wife back from their village, which was close to Kashmir. The journey was rugged, and took him two weeks in all. It took him two days to travel to his village by train, plus another two days walking to his village, and four days repeating that part of the return trip to Karachi. When he returned and learned what Ghulam had been doing, he sat him down and told him that if he were honest and did good work he could always get a good job with Americans.

"But you didn't tell me that," Ghulalm said. "You were here just two days, then you go off to get wife. I thought this big house and nobody check."

Ghulam then kicked Mohammed's puppy "real hard, like a feet ball," Mohammed said. That ended Ghulam's job with us.

After doing my own work for five weeks it was gratifying to discover that I could still manage a household, and still cook, but I was also pleased to learn that I no longer wanted to do so. Not in Karachi.

I spread the word once again that I was looking for a cook. One man applied for the job. After our initial discussion I considered hiring him when he shook his finger angrily at me saying, "Sometimes I no here in time for breakfast; sometimes I no here in time for dinner; and I want no noise about it!"

Who cared about lunch?

After trying out another applicant who proved to be dishonest, he asked me to write him a chit [a letter of recommendation]. I told him, "I can't write you a good chit."

"Well, write me a bad one then!" he said.

Our mali, Azim, continued to be a tremendous help to us. And although he was certainly not a fashion plate—with his bare feet, carelessly wrapped turbans, and lunghies that were usually tucked in at the waist with one leg of the improvised shorts below his knee, the other above the knee—he proved to be a rare jewel, and an artistic one at that.

He adored Joyce, and every once in awhile would build a small house for her out of mud. He would sun bake the mud, then decorate the "house" and it's "yard" with a profusion of flowers. Such was the present he gave her for her fifth birthday on August 31, 1955. Her other presents consisted of being entertained by the usual—a pair of dancing monkeys, a cobra rising out of a jug to a snake charmer's tunes, and a ride on a donkey cart.

Our mali had a gorgeous daughter who was about 12 years old. One day I asked our bearer, "Isn't Azim's daughter beautiful?"

"No, Mem Sahib," Mohammed, who was quite fair-skinned, said. "We peoples think only peoples with skin like yours or mine are beautiful."

The mali's daughter with lovely bronze-colored skin and large, luminous brown eyes, was not considered pretty by Mohammed because of the color of her skin!

Life had reached some degree of normalcy at our new house. In August, 1955, our dachshund, Mem Sahib, gave birth to a litter of Springer Spaniel pups, four little males; and the American Ambassador's daughter, who had married the son of the new Governor General Iskander Mirza the prior year, gave birth to a bouncing baby boy. Both occasions were causes for rejoicing. Had the Ambassador's daughter given birth to a girl, it would have been reason for mourning. Mem Sahib didn't care if she had boys or girls, nor did we. We just thought the pups were darling!

CHAPTER TWENTY-SEVEN

WIDE DISPARITY BETWEEN TWO CULTURES

At midnight on January 18, 1956, Frank and I returned from an eight-day trip to East Pakistan (East Bengal.) It was the first time he had invited me to see one of the projects he had been working on for the Pakistani government and I jumped at the chance to see not only the project, but East Pakistan, the other part of this interesting country.

We left Doug and Joyce in Judi's care, and took a five-hour flight to Dacca, East Pakistan's leading city which is situated 1,000 miles on the other side of India. We registered at the Shahbagh Hotel, and I spent the next couple of days getting acquainted with East Pakistan and getting fat on some excellent hotel food while Frank met with his counterparts.

East Pakistan (Bangladesh) is a lush, semi-tropical country, about the size of Louisiana, that is almost completely underwater six months out of the year. It is as different from West Pakistan as night is from day.

Some 42,000,000 natives crowded together making East Pakistan (also known as East Bengal) one of the most densely populated countries in the world. The people had Asian-like features, ate rice instead of wheat, and spoke Bengali instead of Urdu.

Dacca was a large, overgrown village, not quite as modern as Karachi was (and I use the term loosely), but more as I had expected Karachi to be. The narrow streets were dirty and crowded; filled with bicycle rickshaws, goats, cows, cars, male pedestrians of every description, and automobile horns. I say horns because the drivers seemed to think that the horn was the VITAL part of the car—so vital that if the horn were taken away they would have been at a loss to know how to drive. We saw hardly any women—occasionally a female beggar or sweeper woman, and on rare occasions a woman in purdah. Oxen carts replaced camel carts in East Bengal and tiny Mongolian ponies pulled quaint old-fashioned miniature stage coaches. The people were smaller, less sophisticated, seemed to be more primitive but happier than the West Pakistanis, in spite of the fact that this was cobra country, and wild jackals howled in eerie unison outside of our hotel windows at night.

Two days after we arrived in Dacca, we were driven by Embassy car through some 30 miles of rich farmland to a village named Naranghanj, where we fought our way through hordes of natives and boarded a river boat that took us on the first lap of a trip "up country" to visit the Kopadek irrigation site.

We boarded the boat at 12:30 p.m. and waited on deck for about an hour or so before the boat pulled away. During that time we enjoyed watching the quaint river boats with turned-up bows and sterns glide by. Straw shelters, which were curved and covered the middle of the boats, shielded the occupants from the broiling sun. Closer at hand were natives bathing on a nearby boat, manipulating their lunghies with a dexterity that was amazing. A lunghy is a straight piece of material, about five yards long, worn as an ankle length skirt, and served as the complete ensemble for men. We were fascinated as we watched the community bathhouse in operation on the boat across the way. The natives had a knee-high faucet on the deck, under which they would kneel and wash themselves from head to waist and from foot to thigh while wearing their lunghy. Then, they stepped away from the faucet, put a clean lunghy on and with a flick of the wrist pulled the soiled lunghy off, washed it under the running, murky river water, scrubbed their backs with it, sometimes blew their noses in it, and then squeezed it out and used it as a damp towel to dry off their heads and their bodies. That was the procedure, and fascinated, we watched as endless men repeated the process. Occasionally someone would use soap and jump into the river to rinse, but never once did any of them uncover their private parts.

At about 1:30 p.m. the boat pulled away and we steamed lazily down the river, stopped at every village along the way to load passengers who were rowed out to our boat, or to load fish that were being packed in ice as we waited. Even here, in the river, we couldn't get away from the wallas (the sellers) who rowed their goods—eggs, fruit such as bananas and oranges—out to our boat, boarded it, and attempted to sell their wares. Bananas, a scarcity in West Pakistan, were plentiful in East Pakistan and sold for 2 cents a banana. We made pigs of ourselves eating every banana we could possibly digest.

Fishing and farming were the primary livelihoods of the East Bengalis, and the tropical countryside was peaceful and verdant. Tiny bamboo houses on stilts, four to six feet high, dotted the landscape. If it weren't for the fact that East Pakistan is almost completely flooded six monsoon months out of every year, it would be a far pleasanter place than Karachi in which to live. I realized that I was seeing East Bengal at the best time of the year (Frank had been there when you had to go by row boat to get from one house to the next), but I enjoyed it for what it was at the moment.

Finally, it came time for us to start our journey. We boarded the steamer at 1 p.m. and disembarked the following morning at 4:30 a.m.

With chattering teeth, we walked up a ramp and past hillside fishing/tea shops where even in the darkness, lit only by kerosene lamps, the curiosity of the natives toward Caucasians was not to be denied.

After landing, we walked about half a mile to the other end of a long, British-type train—20 or 30 cars—where we were escorted to a so-called "first-class" compartment. Well, it was private, anyway! The train was dirty and dilapidated, filled to capacity with passengers crammed like cattle inside and out. By "out," I mean countless men were hitching rides by dangling outside of the train windows as it careened down the tracks spewing black smoke over the lush countryside. For three damp hours we shivered and shook with icy noses and cold feet as the train lurched along through the lovely, green meadows.

Finally, dawn became daylight. We fully appreciated the tranquility which prevailed upon the little farm huts that were nestled in groves of banana and palm trees which, in turn, were surrounded by baby palm trees that resembled giant ferns. The huts were built of bamboo with thatched sides and roofs made of palm leaves. They all braved the heavy monsoon weather by being perched on stilts four-to-six feet high. The East Bengalis took advantage of their six-month dry season by growing bananas, mangoes, oranges, grapefruit, pineapple, sugar cane, rice and tea. The scenery was so spectacular we almost forgot how uncomfortable we were. If we were uncomfortable, I wondered, how those poor souls felt who were hanging outside of the train?

Everywhere we looked there were murky ponds filled with water so polluted it was green-gray. Here the natives waded in and caught the fish with little baskets that were about 36" in diameter at one end, and about 9" in diameter at the other end. They slipped the larger end into the water and when a fish was caught, they heard it slap against the sides of the basket and pulled it up from the narrower top.

We arrived at Khustia, our destination, chilled to the bone and glad to get out into the sunshine. We spent three days warming up in Khustia, including one night of that time at the Ganges Kopadek Irrigation site, which was one of Frank's projects.

We were met at the train by two Pakistani engineers who escorted us by Jeep station wagon (a gift of the U.S. Government) to their guest house, where they served us breakfast and mapped out plans for the next two days.

I was fascinated by the trip. Officials of the Pakistani government showed us the Government experimental farm where they had "borrowed" 500 acres of land from the natives to teach them improved methods of farming. They were in the process of digging irrigation troughs, which would be exciting when it was initiated because the farmers had never seen irrigation. Then they took us a little farther where they were showing side by side the difference between local wheat seed and "improved" wheat seed. The improved seed was half again as tall and the Pakistani government was hopeful that by that by demonstrating the difference to the farmers, they would be encouraged to produce more and better crops on their own land. To date, that meant irrigation and improved seed. Period! So far, only the trenches had been dug, and the farmers had not as yet seen any irrigation.

We then drove miles up a road that consisted more by far of ruts than it did of road, to another part of the irrigation canal. The countryside was beautiful; flat and clear, in fact rather barren in the cleared areas, but wherever there was a cluster of palm trees and banana trees, there was a hut; sometimes the hut would be completely, or nearly completely, covered with ivy.

I liked the East Pakistanis a lot. They were without guile; there was no pretense on their parts. All of the little children that we passed were naked except for a little bell or trinket that was tied to a string and hung just below the navel. We were told that this trinket was to keep the evil spirits away. They are put on the children when they are born and are never removed. Ever! The strings are made larger as the children grow, but the trinkets remain until death.

The Jeep was a novelty to the villagers, and everywhere the children would yell and squeal and run from their huts to the roadside to stare. Sometimes we would see girls about nine or ten toiling in the fields. Some of the girls covered their heads with their saris; others threw the saris over their shoulders, leaving their heads uncovered.

"Why do some of the children cover their heads, but others don't?" I asked.

"If their saris cover their heads, it indicates they are married," our guide explained. "When the girls reach puberty, about nine years of age, the girls are married by their parents' arrangement to men anywhere from five years older on up to any age; sometimes to old men who may have had as many as three wives and several children waiting for them at home." As in all Muslim countries, men are allowed to marry four wives.

The people in East Bengal appeared to me to be more primitive than in Karachi. Men wore lunghies such as we had seen on the coolies who were working in our yard when we first moved into the Crazy House. Women wore saris but unlike women in West Pakistan, they usually did not wear cholis (blouses) underneath their saris.

Finally, it came time for us to start our journey. We boarded the steamer at 1:00 p.m. and disembarked about 4:30 a.m. It was pitch dark when we landed, but the twinkling glare of kerosene lamps lit the little tea shops and outlined the curious bystanders who probably had seldom seen Caucasians.

We were able to examine some of the native huts, which were surprisingly clean. Each hut was nestled in a grove of palm and banana trees. Their methods of living were extremely primitive—no sanitation, for example. The ground around the huts was of sun-caked mud or dung that was swept several times a day, leaving a hard surface devoid of debris. As were the refugees in Karachi, these people were too poor to harbor trash. They only owned the clothes on their backs; an earthenware pot or two, and not many more possessions to clutter up their living quarters.

We then visited an irrigation pump that had just been erected. The pump was in the river on sort of a primitive barge, and the pipes were supported by crisscross bamboo poles. The pipe reached to the top of a rather high embankment, and for our benefit the engineer who accompanied us ordered the pump turned on. Within seconds, the ground under our feet was being flooded. I was interested in watching the expressions on the faces of the natives that had gathered around—100 or more who seemed to spring from nowhere as soon as they heard the Jeep. The thing that astounded me was we were seeing history in the making, something truly miraculous in their eyes, and even though they were impressed by the pump and the water, they were more interested in that strange Caucasian woman—that character with white skin; that woman with her face and *legs* uncovered! For the first time I didn't mind being stared at. From the oldest to the youngest they were like simple children, and being such it was easier to understand them.

Later that afternoon we were driven some 16 miles over a nearly impassable road with the Jeep station wagon. It took us a jolting hour to reach the site of the Ganges Kopadek pumping site, and secretly, I was plenty glad when we reached our destination. Apparently I wasn't the only one who felt that way. One of the Pakistani engineers told us about taking his wife on a similar trip a day earlier. "She had to stop midway to rest," he said, "but your American women are stronger."

We stayed that night and the next day in another rest house before visiting the site of the huge Ganges Kopadek pumping site, the first large irrigation project in East Pakistan. Here there were hundreds of natives digging the mud out of the excavation with shovels, toting it out of the pit in baskets on their heads; transferring the baskets to the heads of other coolies who then took the loads about a block away where they dumped the mud. They resembled ants working in chain fashion from where we stood. Labor was still the cheapest thing over there.

We left the project late in the afternoon, drove again to Khustia, where we boarded the train at 11:00 p.m. for a return trip to Dacca, and from there back to Karachi by air.

Shortly after we returned home our mali asked me in some jibberish in Urdu, with a bit of "Amreeks" here and there, so I gathered he wanted to know when we were going to America. I told him, "The end of May." His eyes filled with tears as he said, "Tsk, tsk, tsk—you go Amreeka, me no good; me no good."

The next day we received a letter from him. (Whenever they want us to understand what they are trying to say, they hire a "professional" letter writer who, when squatting in the bazaar, would write it for them.)

To The, Dear, Tessitor Esqr.
Dear, Sir.

Most respectfully & humbly I have draw your kind attention that I am to sad, to hear that your honour, going to your native place after three months.

Because I am very glad to serve your honour and, always, you helped me at every time in need, therefore, kindly, please favour me to serve your honour. I want to say more and anxious to your honor, but it is very sad that I do not speak English well, as, I am to sorry to say some.

Sir, kindly, please give me reply in written.

Your's most obedient servant
Azim (gardener) [sic]

After he handed it to Frank, he stood in the yard and sobbed. He was so fond of Joyce that I knew it would break his heart when we left. As nearly as we could decipher from his letter, he was asking to come with us to the States. I wished it would have been possible.

Shortly afterwards, we learned that Joyce had amoeba. I had suspected it for 1½ years when finally a new doctor arrived from the States and diagnosed her long-standing problem correctly. It was comforting to know that she could now be getting proper medical treatment for her illness

CHAPTER TWENTY-EIGHT

ONE THANKSGIVING; TWO DINNERS

One day, Ishmaili, our artist friend, stopped by to tell us a Pakistani friend of his was returning to Karachi with his American bride.

"I'd appreciate it, Jane, if you would help her get acquainted," he said.

"Lenore," (not her real name) was sweet, naïve, six feet tall, and lacked four hours of having her degree in psychology. Her husband was a few inches shorter, but longer on credits, having just received his PhD degree from the state in psychiatry.

They no sooner were settled in their tiny house when they motored to a village so that Hassan (not his name) could introduce his bride to his wife Number 1, and their five children, all of whom promptly moved in with the newlyweds!

Intermarriage was frowned on by the American community to begin with, but Americans were particularly opposed to that situation. They dropped Lenore like the proverbial hot potato, and spent their time gossiping about "did she know or didn't she know?" She retained her composure and none of us could tell if she had been aware that he had another wife and a bunch of kids and was just being a good sport, or was the revelation a low blow? We never did learn the facts. After a few weeks, wife Number 1 returned to her village, but the five kids stayed on with the newlyweds. I had no idea how long the children stayed.

A few days before Thanksgiving, Lenore stopped by the house to invite us to their house for Thanksgiving dinner.

"We have received a beautiful turkey from the village," she said.

"Oh, Lenore, we would love to but we have already invited some friends to our house for Thanksgiving dinner," I said. We had invited two couples who were our closest friends to join us for the holiday. Noticing her disappointment, I said, "Why don't you and Hassan join us here?"

"That would be wonderful," she said, brightly. "We will bring the turkey."

I arranged to pick the turkey up at their house at 8 a.m. Thanksgiving morning. I was a little apprehensive about springing the news on our friends, but expected them to understand.

They didn't.

One of our friends was aghast. "I thought we were going to have just a quiet 'family' Thanksgiving! I'm sorry, Jane, my husband and I will make other plans."

The other couple bowed out, too, and I was heartsick. I didn't want to offend any of our friends, so I decided to resolve the matter by having two dinners, but not tell any of them what I was doing.

I told Lenore that something had come up with the AID group that we were expected to attend.

"Could we change the dinner to 1:00 p.m.?" I asked. She didn't seem to mind, so we agreed that I would pick up the turkey as originally planned.

I arrived at Lenore's house a few minutes before 8 a.m. and to my horror discovered the turkey strutting around the yard, resplendent with all of its feathers. Furthermore, Lenore and Hassan were sound asleep in their bed—resplendent in their night clothes. I could have choked them!

I rushed home, pulled Frank out of bed, and together we chased the turkey around the yard until we caught it. Frank killed it, but when we got it home, we had to pluck it, eviscerate it, stuff it and cook it by the time our first guests arrived for the 1:00 p.m. dinner. Then we had to hurry up and eat and get them out of the house in time for our second dinner, which was slated for 7:00 p.m. Thanks to Aziz's unwavering skills, we managed, but I don't know how. The joke turned out to be that the turkey from the village was succulent and tender; the one we purchased from the market was tough, stringy and dry. Had our friends been more understanding, they would have had a much better dinner.

To make matters worse, they didn't appreciate the fact that my beautiful lemon pie had slithered off of the serving platter and landed upside down on the terrazzo tile. I picked the pie up carefully, assuring them that none of the filling had touched the floor. To their horror, I then served individual slices of pie with aplomb and apologies! For a long time, we received Christmas cards from one of the guests in which she always mentioned the pie, changing the filling from lemon to apple, to raisin, to pumpkin, and so on, each time. The reminders ceased to be funny after a few years.

CHAPTER TWENTY-NINE

POLITICAL SHENANIGANS, INTRIGUE

It was during our bridge sessions and occasional dinners with Hassan Mahmud and his friends, most of whom were intellectuals and politicians, that we came closest to understanding the political intrigue that was developing within the country. It became more and more evident that there was an air of uneasiness and concern among many of the Pakistanis.

Occasionally we were asked questions that we were hard pressed to answer because we knew nothing about Pakistani politics. Were they testing us? We weren't sure. Sometimes, their conversations would switch to Urdu and furtive glances would be cast in our direction. Behind his back, Mahmud was accused by some as being ruthless and politically ambitious. Others said he would let nothing stand in his way. If so, we were never aware of this side of his character, and it was not our place to pass judgment. Instead, we realized how disillusioned and deeply concerned the Pakistanis were with the problems that beset their country; the impact of Partition, the sorrow, the devastation and problems that occurred—and were occurring—as a result.

It was not the aim or the policy of the U.S. Development Program to dabble in politics; as a matter of fact, it was prohibited. However, one had to be either blind or dead not to realize that there were political shenanigans going on. After we had been in Karachi for several months, we became increasingly aware of tension among more of our friends and acquaintances. Their words became more guarded, and those who had delighted in discussing politics earlier, became hedgy and non-committal.

The reason became clear in October 1954 when the military hierarchy, said to have been engineered by Governor General Ghulam Mohammed, overthrew the faltering, unstable pro-Western government and replaced it with a pro-Western government that this time was a military-controlled dictatorship.

As far as we knew, everything appeared to be normal. The exceptions were the newspapers, which always had been strictly censored, but now were suddenly filled with stories planted (we suspected) by the controlling body to allay any fears that the public had regarding the new regime. As we tried to understand the political developments, we became more interested in the background of the nation and its leaders, both past and present.

When the military coup took place, we were ordered to stay in our homes, and not under any circumstances appear in the street. There were a few minor disturbances (including two cars belonging to Americans that were overturned) but for those of us who followed orders, there was no problem.

Because of the continuous press censorship it was impossible to glean any truth from the news media. Following the coup, we had invited a friend to our house for dinner. This friend, whom we shall call Akbar, was not involved in politics, but over a period of time, we had had many interesting conversations with him and we valued his opinions. During our visit, we broached the subject.

"What caused the coup?" we asked.

"To tell you anything, I shall have to go back to the founding of 'Pawkistawn,' "he said in his clipped English accent. "As you know, in 1947, Mohammed Ali Jinnah founded 'Pawkistawn.' He had been seriously ill for some time but was determined to establish a Muslim country.

"As World War II was coming to an end in May 1945, Britain's labor government was taking steps to grant independence to India. It was apparent that Pakistan and India could not and would not get along. Hatred, which had long been festering between Pakistan and India largely because of religious fanaticism on both sides, clearly revealed that the two countries could not resolve their differences."

Akbar continued his narration explaining that from the eighth century until 1857, the Muslim sultans of Delhi dominated all but the south of India. Three-fourths of the 400,000,000 inhabitants of British India were

Hindus who were against freedom of religion. They refused to accept the Koran and the teachings of Mohammed.

"Muslims and Hindus had lived side by side for centuries in British-ruled India, but seldom intermingled; intermarriage was forbidden," Akram said, taking off his glasses and wiping the lens. "If they dared to intermarry, they were ostracized by both groups." He replaced his glasses carefully, saying "The hatred worsened between the two groups over the years until it became an intolerable situation. We knew that Mohammed Ali Jinnah [also called Quaid-i-Azam, an honor the masses bestowed upon him in 1940 meaning The Great Leader] had been toiling for years to get the Muslims a country of their own. The situation between the Indians and Muslims had become irreconcilable due to the differences in religion, dress, food, and customs after centuries of dissent. There was nothing the two sides could agree upon; there was no way anything would change to make it better. Except Partition. Like a divorce between two dysfunctional people, Partition seemed to be the only solution.

"In the early part of 1947, the state of India asked their Congress to reconsider Partition. Gandhi, a man of peace, could see no other alternative to stop the massacres and bloodshed that was going on.

"Jinnah, who later became the 'father of Pakistan,' charged that a British-Hindu conspiracy was being worked against Muslims. On August 15, 1947 [the day following the start of Partition], he called upon India's Muslims to take things into their own hands if they hoped to create their own country. The Quaid declared the next day 'Direct Action Day,' where their religion predominated in the hopes that they would be sheltered. At the end of the four days, 5,000 people had been killed in the 'Great Calcutta Killing' and an estimated 10,000 were injured.

"Soon all hell broke loose! Pent-up emotions exploded. The hatred that had been simmering for years came to a roiling boil and erupted into what was to become a four-day war in Calcutta. As the four-day battle wound down, the massacre spread like a wildfire into a battle that consumed the Punjab and in between. When Jinnah announced that the end to British rule in India and the beginning of Partition would become effective as of August 15, 1947, huge hordes of people fled their homes in panic. By the time the brutal conflict between the Hindus and Muslims ended almost a year later, 500,000 people had been killed, millions of dollars worth of businesses and property had been destroyed, and the map of British India was changed forever. Hindu India was reduced in size to a country half the size of the United States although it had the second largest population in the world. The 'bastard child', Pakistan, became a new country that was sixth in size and terrain of world states, roughly the size of Utah, Arizona and Nevada combined," Akbar recounted, shifting uneasily in his chair.

CHAPTER THIRTY

A GEOGRAPHICAL ABSURDITY

"The new nation, Pakistan, was carved out of British India according to the preponderance of religion, into two parts so that there was a gigantic wedge—1,000 miles of enemy India—positioned between East and West Pakistan. The two Muslim countries were the unfortunate results of Jinnah's 'win'; they spoke different languages [Urdu and Punjabi], had different customs, ate different foods [rice in the west; wheat in the east]; one country faced east, the other faced west, and there was no land communication between the two.

"Dividing Pakistan in this fashion, 'a geographical absurdity,' was a major flaw in the otherwise brilliant plans developed painstakingly by Jinnah. It made little sense. It was akin to splitting the United States into two parts and positioning an enemy country, 1,000 miles wide, in between California and Maryland.

"The army, the navy, the air force, and the assets of British India, were also divided, with the best of everything going to the Hindus. Soldiers were shared out according to their religion, and suddenly friends turned into enemies. Their guns and ammunition were meted out—two out of three going to the Hindus. The aircraft, and the ships of the Royal Indian Navy, were dealt like a deck of cards according to the religion of the officers and crews. The Muslim ships were handed over to the Pakistanis without a teaspoon of surplus fuel, and when they pulled into the Port of Karachi none of them had any fuel or oil left. Ships had to stay moored at the piers, idle and defenseless."

To say Frank and I were mesmerized during Akbar's recitation was an understatement, but it was also depressing.

"Even worse, authorities divided hospital supplies, and harassed Muslim doctors were aghast when they discovered that most of the supplies and vital parts of surgical instruments had been taken by the Hindus. Medical personnel and technicians had to prepare for the care of thousands of injured and dying refugees with almost no supplies or instruments to treat them. The British divided even such trivial things as typewriters, office furniture and equipment," Akram spat. "The Muslims were more like 'the blue-collar workers' in your country, as opposed to the better educated and upper class Hindus. They lacked the aptitude for business and leadership and were on the losing end of 'one for you and two for me' throughout the entire process. Once they were free they began to settle in villages and towns in their new country of Pakistan only to discover to their dismay that they not only did not have the essential training, but had been given few of the tools that they needed to create their businesses and start their new lives."

"I've never heard how your country came to be called 'Pakistan,'" I said, more to change the subject, then out of curiosity.

"The word Pakistan means the land of Paks, spiritually pure and clean. It is a Persian and Urdu word which symbolizes the religious beliefs and ethnical stocks of Pakistanis, and is derived from the first letters from all of the homelands—that is, Punjab, Afghania [North West Frontier Province], Kashmir, Iran, Sindh [including Kutch and Kathiawar], Tukharistan, Afghanistan and Balochistan."

Akbar was in the process of releasing years of pent—up emotions, and telling us about the horrors that had gone into developing Pakistan seemed to be therapeutic for him. Once he started talking, it seemed to be impossible to turn him off! He was baring his soul, and trying to stop him was like trying to stop the water from spilling out of an overflowing dam.

"Jinnah, the warm-hearted, devout son of gentry, had inherited a gift for leadership and empathy, with no private ambition whatsoever. He had worked unselfishly for years in support of Muslim causes, but it was not until 11 months before September 3, 1939, when war was declared, that his power over the Muslims was recognized and established," Akbar said. "Jinnah's close friend, Liaquat Ali Khan, became his able organizer. Liaquat was a self-made achiever due solely to his fine character and extraordinary talents which complimented Jinnah's. Their solid friendship, nurtured by their incredible honesty and integrity, and their mutual good humor, survived all the ethical hazards of public life until the end.

"Lord Mountbatten, the last Viceroy of India, had, with the help of advisors, developed 'The Plan' that would serve as a guide in transferring British rule in India and returning it to the Indians. In 1944, Jinnah and Mahatma Gandhi met for 18 days attempting to resolve their differences. Jinnah had proposed separating India into two nations, insisting that Muslims 'have their homeland in India same as the Hindus,' Gandhi, by letter, wrote that he thought it was an 'unreal' idea.

"Jinnah was becoming more frail, and although his health was failing, he never stopped working. He responded to Gandhi by writing:

> *We maintain that Muslims and Hindus are two major nations by any definition or test as a nation. We are a nation of a hundred million, and what is more, we are a nation with our own distinctive culture and civilization, language and literature, art and architecture, names and nomenclature, sense of values and proportion, legal laws and moral codes, customs and calendar, history and traditions, aptitudes and ambitions; in short, we have our own distinctive outlook on life and of life.*
>
> *By all the canons of international Law, we are a nation.*

"Gandhi was not prepared to grant Pakistan full sovereignty as implied in the phrase 'sovereign Independent States.' Jinnah considered his proposal an insult and said, 'The fact is, the Hindus want some kind of agreement which will give them some form of control over the Muslims. They will not reconcile themselves to our complete independence.'

"Pakistan was referred to as 'a country fathered by hatred, mothered by poverty, and delivered by the British Parliament.' There would be almost no common ground, although there was a little interchange in architecture and the arts between the Hindus and the Muslims. Britain's Parliament, recognizing the futility of continuing negotiations, in July 1947, finally declared 'from August, 15, 1947, two independent dominions shall be set up in India to be known as India and Pakistan.' From this date, the Indian States would no longer owe allegiance to the British Crown; inhabitants would be completely independent and could choose to remain in India or transfer to Pakistan as they wished. The Hindus and Muslims were overjoyed at their newfound independence, but for the Pakistanis, the birth of the new country was shaky from the beginning.

"We were inspired under Jinnah's leadership, which was straightforward, ethical to the point of being rigid, and absolutely honest. He was often described as being cold and aloof, but his integrity was never questioned. When he died from tuberculosis on September 11, 1948, thirteen months after he founded the republic, the whole nation mourned. It was traumatic. He was our strength, and in him we found our vision. When he died, all of us died a little.

"Jinnah was aware of the complexities of developing a new nation, and immediately recognized the dangers that would face it, particularly in the economic field. For this reason, he appointed Ghulam Mohammed, a 'financial wizard' from Hyderabad, asking him not to be Prime Minister, but to be a civil servant who would make the decisions for a figure-head Prime Minister."

"Ghulam Mohammed? Is he the same person who is now the Governor General?" Frank asked.

"Yes."

"Why wasn't he appointed Finance Minister directly?"

"He couldn't because Ghulam didn't belong to the Constituent Assembly." [The Constituent Assembly was the controlling body responsible for the dual role of law-making and writing the constitution for the new nation.]

"Ghulam Mohammed would have none of this! Ghulam was ambitious—too ambitious, many people felt, and he demanded that he receive the title *and* the responsibility of Finance Minister. Ghulam stubbornly refused to be a surrogate. Because Jinnah's considered opinion was that Ghulam was definitely the best man for the critically important position of Finance Minister, he relented."

"But you said Ghulam didn't belong to the Constituent Assembly," Frank said.

"No, he didn't, but they got around that somehow." Our friend was thoughtful for a moment, then added, "Ghulam was cunning and shrewd—in fact, he had been dubbed 'the big, dangerous cat' in Hyderabad. It wasn't long before his cunning became evident."

"What happened?" I asked, feeling as though we were living an important part of Pakistan's history vicariously.

"Well, it's a long story, but to help you understand, I have to give you a little more background," he continued. "Liaquat Ali Khan, an unusually able politician, was appointed our first Prime Minister by the Constituent Assembly. It was his responsibility to form a government, and in his capacity as Prime Minister he graduated from being an able politician to becoming one of the world's outstanding leaders—on a par with India's Prime Minister Pandit Nehru. Liaquat Ali was kind and his leadership was fair to all. He and Jinnah were idolized by our people. Besides, at this period, during 1951, Pakistan exuded confidence and prosperity with amazing financial strength, due somewhat to the Korean War, but largely to the skill of small, portly Kwaaja Nazimuddin. Nazimuddin, Chief Minister of East Bengal, had been appointed to Governor General as Jinnah's replacement, by King George of the British Empire, upon recommendation of Liaquat Ali Khan. He was a religious man, able and honest with extensive executive experience, but unfortunately he proved to be too weak to successfully handle the problems caused by the unscrupulous anarchy that was threatening to destroy our government.

"Things began to go from bad to worse, to use your expression," our friend said. "Then it became clear that there was trouble brewing between Liaquat Ali Khan on the one side and Ghulam Mohammed and Mushtaq Gurmani on the other.

"You know Gurmani, don't you?" he asked Frank.

"I have met him briefly. I know who he is, that's about all," Frank said, recalling that he was Minister of Kashmiri Affairs, and we had seen him on occasion at official functions.

"Dissension between Ghulalm Mohammed and Mushtaq Gurmani, soon became apparent, even though the newspapers did their best to play down the news. Liaquat Ali decided he had no choice but to address the world and explain Pakistan's foreign policy and also clarify his own views regarding the Kashmiri dispute.

Akbar wiping the perspiration from his face as he struggled to control his emotions, continued. "In March of 1951 a conspiracy to overthrow the government was revealed in Rawlpindi. Liaquat Ali insisted on giving his speech there because that city held the headquarters for army ground forces. Most of the reports referred to differences that he and Ghulam Mohammed had over foreign policy, and they had stemmed from there. Liaquat Ali's position paralleled that of the United States, whereas both

Ghulam and Gurmani supported India's and Britain's desire to take a softer approach toward India in regards to settling the Kashmir dispute.

"Allah abandoned the Prime Minister Liaquat Ali Khan that fateful day," our friend said sadly. "As he approached the speaker's platform, October 16, 1951, Said Akbar, an Afghan native, [no relation] shot and killed him. To make matters worse, the audience captured the assassin, but immediately a police official rushed up and shot the killer. To quote Begum Ali Khan, 'It is a point of conjecture by many of us why it is that even though one official was found to be negligent in his duties, instead of being reprimanded, he was promoted time after time until he became the Deputy Inspector General of Police in West Punjab, the second most important such position in the Province. The Inspector of Police who was also accused of being excessively negligent was promoted to the job of Agent to the Governor General in Baluchistan!'

"Ah, yes," our Pakistani friend said, as his eyes narrowed to slits, "those promotions took place *after* the Cabinet reconstruction of October 1951 Before Nazimmudin could pray to Allah, he was talked into stepping *down* to become Prime Minister in favor of Ghulam Mohammed stepping *up*_to become Governor General. It was said officially that this move was made because Ghulam was in ill health having spent many months recovering from a severe stroke, and the pressures of the higher office would be lessened.

"We've seen the Governor General many times, "I said. "He must have been a very strong leader, but since his stroke, he is just a pitiful shell of a man."

Be that as it may, it is unlikely that Nazimuddin would have agreed to such a move, except for the fact that he didn't expect—nor did anyone—the Governor General to live. Instead of dying, however, Ghulam Mohammed not only lived, but became foxier and more cunning the more immobile he became. This," our friend said, "is where the plot thickens!"

"Don't you fool yourself," our friend said testily. "Beneath this 'pitiful shell' as you put it, lurked a crafty, ruthless fox, eating anybody, especially politicians, who unwittingly stepped into his den. The more physically disabled he became, the more conniving and cunning he was. What he lacked in physical strength, he made up for in shrewdness."

I had heard such remarks before, but discounted them. We saw the Governor General, or G.G. as he was called, occasionally at formal or State affairs. He was always impeccably dressed in traditional Indian garb, straight white trousers instead of the voluminous shalwar trousers that most Muslims wore. Topping the trousers was a long white overblouse, black coat, dark glasses, and a Jinnah cap of Persian wool. He appeared at functions, tottering feebly along with the help of his cane and supported by either Captain Sayeed Khan, or Captain Ozmut Khan, his aides-de-camp, both of whom were friends of ours.

Shortly after the military coup of 1951, the G.G. suffered a severe stroke which robbed him of his physical strength as well as his powers of speech. We attended several functions where he insisted on speaking although no one, not even his closest friends or advisors, could understand a word he said. He was a pitiful sight, and only the oblivious were mislead by the appearance of this once handsome man. Now, he was not only impossible to understand, but he had the glassine appearance of the very ill.

Sipping his tea thoughtfully, Akbar finally said, "Those who studied the situation carefully soon realized that as the G.G.'s physical strength became weaker and weaker, his mind became shrewder and more ruthless."

We were aware that his aides-de-camp, Sayeed and Ozmut, maintained absolute loyalty to their G.G., but through others we heard disturbing facts about his character. We asked Akbar if he had heard any of them.

"Yes, rumors about him were rampant. He was said to be syphilitic. Despite that illness, and his strokes, he drove himself relentlessly, working many 14-hour days. He would walk barefoot in the sand in an attempt to build up his withered leg muscles. He was sometimes seen crying in his room. He was often found worshipping at the image of a Sufi saint, despite the fact that the Muslim religion opposes the worship of idols and saints. He is said to have whiled away many late-night hours drooling over films of voluptuous, sexy girls. Topping the list was Marilyn Monroe."

The conversation abruptly switched to the weather when our cook/bearer brought in some small, fried cakes and freshly baked cookies. After he refreshed our tea and served the refreshments, Aziz left the room, and our friend continued his narrative.

"For the next 18 months, although the situation seemed calm enough on the surface, a crisis was developing between Ghulam Mohammed and

Prime Minister Nazimuddin, resulting in an open break between them after the Lahore riots in March and April of 1953."

"That was just a few months before we arrived," I interjected.

"Yes. This time Nazimuddin called a special meeting and informed his Cabinet that he was aware that the Governor General was planning to have him assassinated. He advised his Cabinet members that he was going to call Queen Elizabeth and ask to have the Governor General removed from office. To the amazement of all, one of Pakistan's Cabinet members was spying for Ghulam. His spy passed the news along to the Governor General, enabling the G.G. to dissolve the Cabinet and form a new one on the spot.

"By coincidence, and many of us wonder how accidental it was, Mohammed Ali, the glamour boy of Pakistani politics and subsequent Ambassador to the United States, just 'happened' to return to Karachi. The G.G. asked him to form a new Cabinet, which he did. It was no surprise that he replaced all of the members who were friendly to Nazimuddin."

Although we arrived in Karachi six years after Partition, we could feel the intense hatred and bitterness that was rampant on both sides. The same old issues existed: dissension over Kashmir, dissension over water rights and dissension over 99 other disputes between the two countries. And of great concern was the relationship that the United States had with India and with Pakistan, and whether democracy or communism would thrive in Asia.

A decision made by the U.S. government to give military arms to Pakistan did nothing to help the situation. Indians were quick to argue that the military arms pact to Pakistan made the United States an enemy of India on the one hand; on the other, India supported the United States in its efforts to suppress communism. In spite of the resentment over the U.S. military aid to Pakistan, we sensed a strong feeling on the part of this sickly nation to *want* to support the West; to *want* to oppose communism. The question was, could it survive? One American sized up the situation by saying, "I don't think our gain in Pakistan will benefit democracies to any great extent. I think military aid to Pakistan is a mistake, not only because of its adverse effect on India, but because we are giving it to a weak, corrupt regime."

Arguments to the contrary, John Foster Dulles and others in Washington were determined that Pakistan could become a strong enough bulwark against the Chinese-Russian communism to justify angering India.

They argued:

1. *Pakistan, with a population of 77,000,000 people and a strong, well-trained army of a quarter of a million men, was a key nation to protect American interests at Russia's back door;*
2. *Pakistan holds the key to the historic Kyber Pass, through which invaders had stormed into the subcontinent for centuries;*
3. *Karachi's port and airport, and airfields in Quetta, Dalbandin, and Pishin, were major soviet targets;*
4. *Pakistan was an important link in an anti-Communist Moslem bloc stretching form Egypt to Indonesia.*

I recalled Frank telling me that during the training he received in Washington, emphasis was made on the importance of giving aid to Pakistan because of its strategic location, and it was the Mutual Security Policy to give aid on a quid pro quo basis—in other words in this case, we will provide aid; you provide a bulwark against communism.

However, Pakistan, the new country situated in the Indus Valley where one of history's oldest civilizations thrived hundreds of years earlier, was close to bankruptcy; the economy was so shaky, it was impossible to support building an army. There was little surplus money to provide for social services like education or health, because most of the bare necessities of life, food, clothing and shelter consumed most of their income.

Many Pakistanis blamed Western domination and economic exploitation for Asia's plight. "Why must Asians be impoverished in the midst of plenty?" Chaudhri Mohammed Ali, Pakistan's Finance Minister, said in 1955. "The tension created by the big powers is largely responsible for this country's pressing poverty. We live in a world environment where even poor countries have to buy tanks and airplanes to defend themselves. An undue proportion of their resources is spent on defense. This is but one of the penalties imposed for being underdeveloped in an industrially advanced world." He continued by saying, "Why shouldn't we be worried about Western imperialism? The political exploitation has ended but the economic exploitation continues."

"We need your help desperately", a Pakistani told us. "We are one of the world's poorest countries. Your country is rich. A family of five in our country earns an average of $200 (U.S.) per year—one–twenty-fifth of the economy of the United States!"

"That's hard to imagine," I exclaimed, but remembering the thousands of refugee huts honeycombed throughout the city, I realized there might be a great deal of truth in his statement. In fact, an official Embassy Report from February 1954 stated that 88% of the people in Pakistan live on a salary of less than $55 a year!

"Why, right here in Karachi, 52% of the population are refugees. Most of them are tradesmen and laborers—blue-collar workers as you would say; most of the Hindus are the so-called white-collar workers. This disparity, by nature of the two religions, presents a problem in establishing a strong economy."

Whenever we could encourage Pakistanis to discuss their personal experiences when they fled their homes in India to their new nation, their answers were filled with pathos and bitterness.

"There was bloodshed and unbelievable cruelty," Akbar recalled. "The violence spread across the sub-continent like a horrible disease, and many of our friends and relatives were among those who were killed or violated. Our friend was obviously shaken as he relived those horrible moments, forgetful of time, but not forgetful of his hatred toward the Indians as he recounted his personal trauma, and his country's nightmare.

"How did you escape to Pakistan?" we wondered.

"We walked for days. We crawled along at night, sneaking from one dark corner to another; sleeping in standing positions in some cases, on the ground in others. We were forced to leave all of our belongings behind, except my mother managed to secrete her jewels by sewing them in her undergarments." Tears welled up in his eyes, and rolled down his cheeks. With great effort, he continued. "She wasn't clever enough, though. They found the jewels, then raped her and left her for dead. She was 67 years old."

He wept openly now, then regaining his composure, went on. "Bodies were stacked all over the countryside, in the cities, the streets, the rivers, and they were even clogging the sewers. The stench was sickening.

You can imagine what happens to bodies when they are stacked in hot, humid temperatures," He shuddered visibly. "Many of the bodies were bloated, and looked more like balloons than people. You see, this was August, and the temperatures hovered around 107 degrees."

My heart went out to him and to his family. Occasionally others would volunteer to relate similar experiences, but I never pressed the subject because it was too painful for them. I could only thank God that I was an American, and had had the good fortune to avoid such cannibalism.

CHAPTER THIRTY-ONE

NEFARIOUS BUT TALENTED

The past three years of our tour in Pakistan had passed quickly, and now we were preparing to return home.

The sun beat unmercifully upon Karachi, as was its custom in May, causing the occupants of the city to retreat into the coolest corners for their afternoon siestas, especially now during Ramazan, the fasting month. I had dashed down to the American Embassy to attend to last minute details when the receptionist, an attractive Anglo-Pakistani woman in her late forties, stopped me in the hall and said, "You go America soon? You have clothes to sell?"

"Yes, I do," I replied. "As a matter of fact, I am running an ad in tomorrow's newspaper. If you are interested, you had better look them over before the paper is published."

"Yes, I come 1:00 this afternoon, O. K.?"

"O.K.", I said smiling, happy at the prospect of selling some of our things.

At exactly 1:00 p.m. the doorbell rang, and to my surprise the visitor was not the receptionist, but the woman I had seen her in deep conversation with at the Embassy earlier in the morning.

"Excuse me, Mrs. Tessitor, Mrs. Khan could not make your appointment, but since the clothes are for me, I thought you would not mind if I came alone," Mrs. Khan's friend said.

Our visitor was a most attractive Pakistani woman, unusually friendly, with an American accent rather than the usual British accent. She was in her mid-forties, or thereabouts, I surmised, but I could never be sure because Pakistani women carried their ages so well. She introduced herself as Begum Habib. I was impressed with her at once. She was pleasingly plump and was smartly groomed in an azure blue sari, silver filigree jewelry at her wrists and her ears, and on her feet were the traditional t-strap sandals worn by the upper class women. Her jet black hair was parted in the middle and pulled straight back over her ears and fashioned into a bun at the back of her neck. Her eyes were lovely, outlined entirely with surma, as was the custom, giving them a darker and more lustrous look.

"I hope you don't think I am too presumptuous, but my friend, Kathleen, told me you are going to the States soon, and will have some things to sell."

"Not at all," I said. "What are you interested in, Begum?" I asked.

"I am particularly interested in clothes, but would like to see what else you will be selling," she said. "It is so difficult for us Pakistanis to buy American goods, and as you know, if we buy them on the open market they are so frightfully expensive.

"I know your difficulties in this respect," I said, sympathetically. Import duties were high, and American products were respected and highly coveted. Unless of course, they had been completely ruined by the servant's misuse, which wasn't unlikely.

Begum Habib examined a few of the garments carefully, then exclaimed with her eyes shining brightly, "What marvelous quality! These garments are lovely, and so reasonably priced, too!"

Putting aside a pair of slacks and then a cocktail dress, Mrs. Habib continued, "It is so sad, but so many Americans charge so much for their goods, it is simply prohibitive for us to buy them."

Doug and Judi were helping me with the sale. She glowed at us. We had tried so hard to be fair and I was glad that she appreciated our efforts.

Begum Habib sorted through all of the clothing, frequently praising either the goods or the prices. As she was doing so, she confided that she was buying the clothes for some orphans that were supported entirely by a Guild to which she belonged.

"We believe in taking care of our own," she said proudly.

That's a switch, I thought to myself, as Doug and Judi rolled their eyes. We had enjoyed knowing the Pakistanis during our three-year tour, even though our stay had not been without frustrations, but taking care of their own less fortunate was hardly a quality for which they were known.

We liked Mrs. Habib more all of the time. We seemed to have an instant rapport with her. It was easy for us; we were naturally friendly and related well with people of other races, but I especially enjoyed the talkative Mrs. Habib who was so much at ease in a stranger's home. I admired her immensely for her compassion towards her own less fortunate. Besides, hadn't she bought nearly all of the clothes?

She spent the remainder of the afternoon examining everything else that was for sale. She could hardly contain herself! To say she was ecstatic was putting it mildly.

"Your prices are marvelous," she kept repeating as she bought all of the kitchen pots and pans, dishes and flatware; the appliances; the toaster; the mixer and the transformers that accompanied them. As she neared the sink, she asked if she might have a glass of water. I started to get it for her since our servants had not yet returned from their afternoon siesta, but Mrs. Habib said, "Never mind. I'll help myself, thank you," and to my surprise, she reached for a glass and helped herself to the water from the faucet in the low Pakistani sink.

Her enthusiasm as she shopped from room to room astounded and pleased me as I watched her put aside countless articles with help from Judi and Doug—children's toys, knick knacks, bedding and the like.

"No, I don't need a sewing machine, my dear, but I have a friend who does need one. I'll send her to you the first thing in the morning as I am sure she will be interested in most of the things that I don't select."

As the Begum examined the tennis rackets, I reflected on the happy hours Frank and I had spent on the nearby court that was paved with camel dung. It was hard as asphalt when the weather was dry but when the monsoons arrived, it was another story! I was aroused from my thoughts when Mrs. Habib put the rackets with the other things she was buying and asked if she could get herself another drink of water.

Returning from the kitchen she noticed the silver hollowware tea and coffee service, and our Lenox china that were visible in the china cabinet and asked if they were for sale.

"I'm sorry," I said. "I don't want to sell those."

"Oh, but you *MUST*, my dear! It is impossible for us to buy such things, and I need them so badly. I am moving into a new apartment and I will need to furnish it completely from the beginning."

I finally relented and reluctantly agreed to sell her our sterling flatware, too. Mrs. Habib seemed to be becoming increasingly nervous. She helped herself to several more glasses of water, and began to pace nervously about the floor. I noticed this change in her demeanor, but rationalized the

Begum's actions as a result of the excitement of finding so many things that she wanted to buy. Sort of the way we feel at home after a morning in Macy's bargain basement, I imagined.

I began reflecting on Mrs. Habib's independence. It was so unusual because the upper-class Pakistani women don't lift a finger to do menial things for themselves. Servants are cheap and the women are accustomed from birth to being waited on, but Mrs. Habib insisted on helping herself. Probably because she had lived in the States for seven years, I decided. Also, her accent was refreshingly American as compared to the usual clipped British accent of the other Pakistanis I had known. When I commented on this to the Begum, she laughed and explained that she had graduated from Northwestern University in Chicago.

She told us a lot about her background. She had lived in Chicago for a number of years and she said her brother was well known by Frank.

"I love the States. I wish I could go back there to live, but I have a family here, you know. As a matter of fact, my husband knows your husband. They work together, in fact. My husband is the official counterpart of the Pakistan government to your husband."

"Amazing!" I exclaimed. "It's a small world, isn't it?" Frank had never mentioned her husband, but then that was not unusual. He seldom brought his work home.

It was 6:30 p.m. now. The afternoon had flown by quickly and my visitor excused herself. She returned in a few minutes, apologized for leaving and said, "I'm sorry. I released my driver. It is Ramazan, you know, and he has been fasting without food or water since sun-up this morning. I have kept him much too long. He must return to his home as it is beginning to be dark and he will have to break his fast. Would you be good enough to drive me to Clifton Heights?"

"Well, yes, of course," I answered, not a little shocked at her boldness. Clifton Heights was way on the opposite side of town from our house, and she seemed to have no concern that she might be imposing on me. "We have sold our car, so I'll have to drive you there in the Jeep."

"That will be fine. It's just that I would like to bring the clothes back with me tonight and I dislike taking a taxi with all of those clothes."

I understood her position, and reluctantly complied.

"Now before I go, Mrs. Tessitor, how would you like to have me pay for these things?" I had made a list as we went along of all of the items that Mrs. Habib had purchased, and the amount came to US $2,126. "Do you want me to give you a check, or may I give you a letter to the manager of my bank? I always do business that way in order to avoid taxes. Mr. Kybeer is a friend of mine and it is much simpler that way."

Again, I was shocked. I had never heard of doing business in that fashion, but then, this was Pakistan, and everything seemed to be done differently—no rhyme nor reason for it. I finally agreed, against my better judgment.

After she had written the letter, I showed it to Frank, who had remained out of sight in the comfort of the one air-conditioned room in the house during the entire transaction. He glanced at the letter and shrugged. He, too, had never heard of this method of doing business, but nodded his assent. "It's O.K., I guess."

I summoned our mali who helped put the clothes in the Jeep. Mrs. Habib and I piled in with the clothes and headed across town. First, we stopped at a petrol station because the Jeep was low on gas. Suddenly, Mrs. Habib gasped and hid her face in her hands. "See that man over there? He is a friend of mine."

Why did she turn her face away if he were a friend of hers, I wondered? As if reading my mind, Mrs. Habib continued, "I don't want him to see me. You see, he owes me some money, and it would only embarrass him." That was considerate of her, I thought.

The sun had slipped behind the horizon now, and darkness was settling quickly upon the two of us as we drove slowly through Karachi, behind camel carts, dodging bicycles, jinrikshas, and pedestrians. Then we waited—waited for what seemed to be an eternity—for a herd of buffalo to amble across the street.

"I'm going to miss Karachi," I said, breaking the silence. It's like being in another world, almost like Biblical times." Mrs. Habib nodded, but didn't respond.

We finally arrived at her address. She bade me stay in the Jeep saying, "I'll go call my driver to fetch the clothes." Within a few minutes they both returned. After the driver unloaded the clothes, Mrs. Habib thanked me profusely and they slipped away into the darkness of the Pakistani night.

The next, morning I was forced to turn away hordes of would-be buyers who were at the door bright and early in answer to the ad. It was such a relief to have been able to sell my things so effortlessly, I thought. Soon Mrs. Habib's friend would arrive to buy the rest of the goods we had for sale, and I could forget all about selling and busy myself with more important details.

Funny, it was already noon and her friend had not yet arrived, nor had Mrs. Habib come for the rest of the things she said she wanted to buy. I dismissed an uneasy feeling in my stomach but it kept returning like the plague. By late afternoon, my stomach felt like a jelly fish struggling to escape.

I began to brood. "I wonder," I said, half out loud. Obviously I hadn't read the letter very carefully. "Do you suppose," I said, as I rose to find it. My worst suspicions were confirmed! To my dismay, this is what the letter to the bank said:

> To the Manager
> Natl. Bank of Karachi, Ltd.
>
> Please give the bearer of this letter the amount of Rs. $86,680
> from my account.
>
> Signed,
> Begum Ahmed Habib

My God! The manager had no name! There was no bank account number. I reread the letter in disbelief. Hoping that my faith in human beings would be restored, I was determined to check on Mrs. Habib's account at the local bank the first thing in the morning. My heart sank. The next day was Friday, the Muslim Sabbath, and the banks would be closed until Saturday.

I was waiting dejectedly at the bank Saturday morning at 9 a.m. and was promptly ushered into the manager's office. He was tall and strikingly handsome, straight as an arrow, with a luxuriant beard and beautifully chiseled features. He could easily have qualified for the Governor General's bodyguards, I thought. He offered me a seat and I quickly began explaining my predicament.

"Tell me," I began, "Does Begum Ahmed Habib have an account at this bank?"

Reluctant at first to divulge a customer's private business, he acquiesced when I explained the circumstances that prompted my concern. He rang the buzzer and rattled off some orders in Urdu. Within seconds, a messenger brought in some records. My heart sank as one after another of the huge books failed to confirm the authenticity of Mrs. Habib's account.

Closing the last book, he stood at his full height, and apologized.

"I'm sorry, Begum. We have no account in her name, nor have we ever had one."

The room spun around as I realized that I had been royally duped. How stupid of me, I groaned to myself. This whole thing was just plain idiotic. I felt sick to my stomach. My nausea turned first into anger at my stupidity, then into anger at Mrs. Habib's dishonesty. Furious, more at myself than at Mrs. Habib, I made an appointment to see the Consul General of the American Embassy. He listened intently, puffing on his pipe as he sat behind his huge teakwood desk listening to me blurt out my story.

"Same old song and dance, I'm afraid," he said.

"Describe her to me." I complied in detail.

"Does she drive a huge green Cadillac?" he asked.

"My mali said she did. I didn't see it," I replied.

"Well," he puffed, "if it's any comfort to you, we know this gal. She is notorious. She has bilked countless Americans out of their possessions; high-ranking people, too. Why only three months ago, she got away with more than $2,000 worth of goods belonging to the USIS [U.S. Information Service] director, and I could give you a list as long as your arm of other people she has defrauded. Influential people they were, too." He blew some smoke rings above his head, and finally, closing his file, he slammed his fist on the desk and bellowed "Call the security guard at the Embassy and see what he can do. I don't hold out much hope, though," he added. "It's a delicate situation trying to force something like this in a foreign country; extremely delicate." He tapped the bowl of his pipe on his ash tray and wished me luck as I rose to leave.

The security guard was a massive, rugged man with a scar on one cheek, thinning hair, rosy features and a puffiness indicating a fondness for alcohol. His feet were planted carelessly on his desk as he listened to my story; which by now had become a nightmare more than a story.

The security guard studied a tiny salamander that was scurrying up and down the walls. It finally disappeared behind the plate at the base of the ceiling fan that was grinding noisily overhead as I spoke.

"Hell, Ma'am, there ain't a damn thing we kin do! She's elusive, that one. Foxy as hell. We've been on her tail for years and have never even gotten close."

Jumping to his feet, he said, "There's jest one thing I kin think of that jest *MIGHT* work. We kin try working through her friend, the receptionist, see?"

I didn't.

"I'll call her in and scare the hell out of her. I'll threaten her with her job. Tell her it's her fault this con went to your place to begin with. I'll scare the bejesus out of her—and wa'al, like I say, if it works, it works. If not, there's not a damn thing we kin do."

I left the security guard's office in low spirits, although it was some consolation to know that I was not alone in having been swindled. The cost of the clothes only amounted to a little over $500, which was of itself not that important, but I had lost the chance to sell the other items which Mrs. Habib had pretended to want. That, too, wasn't nearly as devastating as my hurt pride.

The security guard kept in close touch with us and told us the receptionist was almost hysterical. Three days had passed and she had turned Karachi upside down trying to locate Mrs. Habib to no avail. The deadline they gave the receptionist was quickly approaching and she feared for her job. Not even through that fantastic native grapevine had she found a single clue to her friend's whereabouts.

The pieces were beginning to fall into place, however, and had I not been so directly concerned, I might have found them interesting. I learned that the woman's name was Begum Nazir Malik, whose husband was a well-respected doctor in Karachi (not an official counterpart of Frank's as she had said). Her husband had, in fact become so upset at her actions and the loss of face she had heaped upon their family, that seven months earlier he had kidnapped their children and fled with them to East Pakistan, and he had not been heard from since.

The biggest piece of the puzzle landed like a bomb. I was doing some last minute shopping in Bori Bazaar when a heavily-made, seductive-looking prostitute wiggled past me toward an American tourist. I could not believe my eyes! *She was poured into one of my dresses!* I clasped my hand over my mouth to stifle a scream, then quickly alerted a Pakistani policeman who was standing nearby. Luckily, he spoke a little English—enough that he understood the gist of my problem. He beckoned me to follow him, and together we furtively followed the street-walker past coolie women spreading gravel upon a road; past stalls of Kashmiri handicrafts, inlaid brass and ivory; past stalls of hand-painted pottery and lacquer ware; past street vendors, tattered beggars, persistent hawkers and hordes of pitiful dregs of society. Surely, these creatures were on the trash heap of life.

It was dusk now but we continued our mission as she hurried along. I jerked with a start as a beggar woman clutched at my skirt. She was huddled under a dupatta (stole) with ravages of leprosy visible beneath one corner of it. Further observation revealed that she had lost one half of her face and most of her arm from the disease.

"Bucksheas, Mem Sahib, Bucksheas." she whined, from her squatting position on the ground.

We were well within the bowels of the Old City where Americans are strictly forbidden to go. Thank God the constable was protecting me. I was well aware that white slavery was prevalent in this area, and shivered as I contemplated the danger of walking alone in this slum area.

Finally, there was a horrible stench. A benjo ditch. The streetwalker jumped across it and ducked into a doorway of a nondescript building. She pulled aside a red curtain and stepped inside with the officer bursting in behind her. They had entered the brothel where she worked!

The officer loudly demanded to see the Madame, who turned out to be none other than Begum Habib, aka Begum Malik! He freed the terrified prostitute who was cowering in the corner, but arrested Madame Malik on the spot with a great deal of ceremony. The gathering crowd cheered when handcuffs were snapped onto her wrists and clapped when she was loaded into the waiting patrol wagon.

The Security Guard later called me into his office where I identified the Madame. To all appearances she wasn't going to be bilking anyone else out of anything for quite some time.

The last we saw of her driver was when he raced for a taxi (the Cadillac had been repossessed for non-payment of bills) and our mali was hot on his heels in wild pursuit in the hopes of getting back some of our proceeds from the dresses that she had stolen.

To my chagrin, no legal action was taken against Begum Malik because of the red tape involved, but she was so frightened that we suspected she would probably lay low for awhile.

I secretly felt relieved and a little proud that I had had something to do with her capture. Although my reasoning was different than it had been the first day I met her, I still couldn't help but be impressed with Begum Habib. She was a very talented woman. Nefarious perhaps, but talented. As for me, I learned even in Pakistan you don't do business by writing a letter to the manager of a bank!

CHAPTER THIRTY-TWO

BON VOYAGE

I busied myself with packing for our trip back to the United States with very little time to worry about how Begum Malik was liking her sojourn in the Pakistani jail. I fumed because we were forced to ship some things that I had hoped to sell, but couldn't because Begum Malik had asked me to put them aside because she said she was buying them. I also gloried in the realization that we still had a number of things that I had agreed to sell her, albeit reluctantly.

Among the items that we were sending to the states was Mem Sahib, our dachshund dog. She had to be duly quarantined after which we received a paper entitled:

ISLAMIC REPUBLIC OF PAKISTAN]
CAPITAL OF THE FEDERATION]
CITY OF KARACHI] SS
EMBASSY OF THE UNITED]
STATES OF AMERICA]

May 24, 1956

I, Jane Tessitor, swear that Mem Sahib, my Dachshund bitch has been inspected with (sic) the past ten days and was apparently free of demonstrable diseases involving emaciation, lesions of the skin, nervous system disturbances, jaundice, diarrhea or any other diseases.

She was vaccinated on May 18th with Pittman Moore rabies vaccine.

She was examined by Dr. Rizvy, Veterinary Officer for the Government of Pakistan in Karachi, Pakistan, on May 18th, 1956.

Mrs. Frank Tessitor

Subscribed and sworn to before me this 24th day of May, 1956

Thomas N. Metcalf, Jr.
American Vice Consul

This document got Mem Sahib out of the country legally, but what it didn't do was calm her fears. She had an inherited phobia about being locked up or left alone, and being locked up in a crate was more than she could tolerate. Although hating to be locked up or left alone is characteristic of the dachshund breed, being imprisoned in the "swimming pool" when we were in India, didn't help her emotional state either. Because I was aware of her paranoia, I worried about how she would deal with her confinement during her flight to the States. Rightly so, because by the time she arrived at my sister's house in Altadena, California, there was evidence that she was in a different crate from the one she started out in, and the second crate had been repaired at least once. She had clawed and chewed her way across the Atlantic. She was paranoid; no one knows how many times either of the crates had to have been repaired. My sister found out the hard way about her paranoia when she tallied up the number of times they had to have their new carpet repaired as she desperately tried to claw her way out of Carol's house when left alone.

Shortly before we left Karachi, we had a surprise visit from Ozmut and Sayeed. They came to urge us to bet on a horserace that Ozmut was riding in the next day. Ozmut was a superb horseman. He and Sayeed were members of the elite Governor General's Bodyguard, which gave mounted displays for visiting dignitaries and important occasions at the bodyguard lines to which we were frequently invited. The mounted displays consisted of a variety of exhibitions such as musical rides, Governor General's carriage with postillions in full dress, individual horsemanship exhibitions, show jumping, tent pegging on horseback, wrestling on horseback; relay races and others. The tent pegging was especially thrilling to us as the riders charged at full speed and speared wooden pegs that were stuck in the ground. The riders were amazing. So it was that we were taken in by Ozmut when he declared excitedly:

"I'm riding Major Majid's horse," Ozmut said, "and I'm riding him to WIN! You can't miss! You've got to bet on him! He is a sure winner!"

"He is a wonderful Arabian steed," Ozmut said, "He can't lose! There is no way he will lose!" He continued praising the merits of the horse (and the steed was a beauty!). He urged us to bet and gave us two tickets to the race. Neither Frank nor I were bettors, but because Ozmut was so persistent (and we wanted to please him) we bet $100 on Major Majid's horse to *WIN*, secure in the knowledge that he would place first. We also found it difficult to turn our friend down.

The horses had been exercised, saddled and paraded around the track, and were now lined up in the stalls waiting for the race to start. The bugle blew; the gates opened, and all of the horses charged out—*ALL* except Major Majid's horse. What on earth! We couldn't believe our eyes. He was bucking like crazy, and Ozmut appeared to be trying to control him as the horse pranced and bucked furiously. *The horse never got out of the stall!* As far as we know, he may still be there. We were stunned! Betting on him had clearly been a ruse and, for whatever reason, we had been taken for fools by someone we had considered a dear friend. With our tails between our legs we limped home dejectedly, and drowned our sorrows in martinis over a game of bridge. Sadly, that was the last time we saw our friend, Ozmut.

It was difficult for Doug and Judi to be torn away from their friends once again as we prepared to return to the States. In Doug's case, he had been spending an inordinate amount of time in the bathroom—combing and recombing his hair, and paying a great deal of attention to his grooming.

"What is it with Doug these days?" I whispered to Judi.

"He's in love!" she whispered back.

Judi knew what being "in love" was like because she was hurting over a lost love. A boy she was fond of braided a bracelet out of strips of paper and gave it to her as a token of his affection for her. One day our servant announced that there was a boy in the living room who had come to see her. Her "love" had sent his brother to ask for the return of the bracelet!

Judi was heartbroken. He had dropped her for a charming newcomer, and didn't have the courage to tell her to her face.

I spent hours in my mind reliving experiences that we had enjoyed (or not) as I readied our goods preparatory to getting them packed. I knew I would miss the fractured English of our servants, such as our dhobi telling us his "mother died the day after tomorrow," and his "twelve-year-old daughter was getting married last year." Our dear, sweet mali was so special. One day he said, "Tenk you, Mem Sahib. Tenk you, tenk you. My Mem Sahib King." A few days earlier, in an attempt to compliment me he said, "My Mem Sahib Mommy!"

I would miss the chief Muezzin calling the faithful to prayer. The vocal call to prayer was prescribed by Mohammed because he didn't like bells; the tall minarets on four corners of every temple from which muezzins cry were developed after Mohammed's time. Mohammed was largely responsible for advancing the status of women. It was he who had condemned the killing of baby girls; and he who taught that boys and girls were gifts from God.

I busied myself with the chores at hand, all the while fuming at Begum Malik. Many items that we had to ship home were things that we had hoped to sell, and could have, if Begum Malik had not said she was buying them. Even though there were lots of goods that I didn't want to take home, there were a few items such as our silver plate coffee and tea service, our sterling silver flatware, and our Lenox china that I was glad she had not taken after all.

We were shipping our household goods to Berdina and Wayne's house in Denver. Reminiscent of the experience I had with the packers as we headed for Karachi, I assured Berdina that a box would be arriving at their house, but it wouldn't be very big.

"It won't be very big because we sold a lot of our things," I told her in all innocence as I packed clothing, leftover canned goods, liquor, gifts, pots and pans, and the myriad things a household accumulates. By the time a box was built around these items, it was huge; so huge that the Denver movers couldn't move it. They had to bring in another firm to do so. Once the second firm managed to deliver the box to Hotaling's house, they couldn't get it into the basement; it had to be "parked" in their garage until we could arrive to unpack it. I decided by that time that I was through estimating the approximate size and/or weights of shipments. It was a cinch no one would hire me to give clients packing estimates!

Finally, we were on our way. After saying farewell to our Karachi friends, Frank and I and our children toured Europe and five weeks later sailed for the United States on the newly christened *UNITED STATES* luxury liner from La Harve, France, to New York. The liner was the fastest ship on the seas at that time (33 knots per hour), and we (and former President Harry and Bess Truman and others) arrived in New York three days later. We were soon back in Denver unpacking the "stuff" from our huge box that had been parked in Hotaling's garage, all the while reminiscing about the incredible three years we had experienced in Pakistan. We were grateful to be back in America; grateful to be home.

GLOSSARY

AID—Agency for International Development
Anna—Pakistani monetary unit valued at 1/16 of a rupee
Arabian camel—single hump
Bactrian camel—double hump
Bearer—head servant
Beetlenut—a nut chewed by many that stained their teeth red
Benjou—open air ditch used for human waste
Burqua—a tent-like garment worn by women in purdah
Chappatis—unleavened bread similar to tortillas
Cholis—blouses
Chowkidar—night watchman; guard
Dohbi—laundryman
Dupatta—stole
Durzee—tailor
FOA—Foreign Operations Administration
Hamal—second servant; bearer or cook/bearer's helper
Hookah pipe—a water pipe used to smoke tobacco
Kamiz—long blouse, or long shirt
Lunghies—five yards of material worn by men as a skirt
Kraits—poisonous snakes
Mali—gardener
Mem Sahib—Mrs.
Pan—tobacco
Purdah—Muslim custom requiring women to cover their entire bodies, even their faces, in public
Pye-dogs—wild dogs
Rupee—Pakistani monetary unit worth about 33 cents
Sahib—Mr.
Salaam alaykum—greeting meaning hello, peace unto you

Shalwar—full pants (slacks) worn by most Muslim men
Walla—vendor, salesman
Suma—black soot-like cosmetic worn to outline the eyes
Sweeper—lowly servant on the caste system
Zamindar—large land owner

Made in United States
North Haven, CT
15 November 2021

11160610R00129